Norman Pittenger

AFTER DEATH
Life in God

SCM PRESS LTD

236.22

334 00030 0

First published 1980 by
SCM Press Ltd
58 Bloomsbury Street London

Photoset by Input Typesetting Ltd
and printed in Great Britain by
Richard Clay (The Chaucer Press) Ltd
Bungay, Suffolk

In memory of my parents,
Charles Henry and Clara Louise Pittenger,
and of my brother and sister,
Beatrice Eleanor and Archibald,
dead long since but not forgotten,
safe in God's life for ever

Contents

Preface

There comes a time for all of us when we must reckon seriously with the plain fact that we are going to die. Perhaps most of us, much of the time, can evade this thought; certainly contemporary funeral customs do their best to conceal it from us. Yet death is inescapable – like taxes, as the old saying has it. And since it is inescapable, we have every reason to face up to its reality and come to terms with it, so far as we are able.

One of the ways in which the dread fact of death has been made less important, for a great many people at any rate, has been by talk about 'life after death'. Some have honestly admitted that the basic reason for their faith in God, however God be conceived, is that such a faith will guarantee – or so they believe – precisely such an 'after-life' not only for themselves but for those whom they love and whose loss has been so tragic and disturbing. Indeed, when one reads a good deal of writing about religion, one discovers that belief in the reality of God *and* belief in such a 'life after death' seem to be linked together.

At the same time, we find that many of our contemporaries are honestly doubtful about any such post-mortem existence, although they may genuinely have faith in a divine reality, supremely worshipful, taken to be utterly loving and the guarantee of the worth or value of human existence. Questioning about 'life after death' does not necessarily lead to sheer atheism, or denial of God altogether; nor yet to agnosticism, or uncertainty about whether there is or is not an unsurpassable reality appropriately called God. The ancient Hebrews were in that case: they believed most firmly in God but they did not, in the days up to about two or three centuries

ix

before Christ, have any genuine belief in 'life after death' save in the attenuated sense associated with 'Sheol' – where the ghosts of the departed seem to have had a vague and insignificant continuation. It is easy to see, from a reading of such Old Testament references, that such a continuation of bare existence carried little hope and made little appeal to the ordinary Jew of the time. It was only in the period of the Maccabean revolt that any conception of life 'beyond death' was envisaged as a corollary of belief in a God who was just and who would recompense his people for the suffering they experienced under persecution and slaughter. Yet all the way through their history, the Jewish people were outstanding for their faith in the reality of Yahweh, in his goodness, and in his concern for his human children.

Now I myself grew up in the atmosphere of fairly conventional 'Catholic' piety about matters like this. Death, judgment, heaven, hell, and purgatory were part of the conventional picture. When one died, there would be a 'particular' judgment; at the 'end of the world', there would be a 'general judgment'. Those who were irremediately evil would be assigned to a place (if that was the right word) where God's absence would be felt with everlasting anguish and where condign punishment for wrong-doing would be experienced. Those who had in them the possibility of redemption would be given cleansing or purification in an intermediate state – purgatory was the cosmic 'laundry', as one might put it. Then, after this cleansing, such persons would be permitted to enjoy the vision of God. The saints, or those who in this life had attained perfection, would already be in heaven – and the Blessed Mary, queen of the saints, had long since been established there in glory, next to her Son on his throne. One could pray for the departed, that they might have 'eternal rest' and 'a place of light, refreshment, and peace'; and one could address petitions to the saints, chiefly to the Blessed Mary, who in their generosity would delight in aiding those who were still in the realm of finite existence to grow in grace and become worthy companions in the heavenly abodes.

As the years went by and as I myself became a 'professional' theologian engaged in teaching future clergymen, I found that this neat scheme, in which I had happily grown up, presented problems and raised serious difficulties. In consequence, I was obliged to think through what was *really* being affirmed and what Christian faith must *necessarily* assert as implicit in religious conviction.

But what, then, could I say and think about these matters? How could a contemporary Christian believer understand all existence, so that the living God remained central to his or her life, even though the conventional kind of talk about 'life after death' had little if any meaning? Or to put it more strongly, what could still be said when to that believer much if not all such conventional talk seemed ill-founded, often highly self-centred, and lacking any serious religious value?

In this book I attempt to discuss this subject. I do it from what might be styled a double perspective. First, I write as one who finds himself entirely trustful, so far as God is concerned. My strong conviction is that this God is self-disclosed in the total event of Jesus of Nazareth – and is there disclosed as nothing other than 'pure unbounded Love', as Love-in-act, as (if you will) the cosmic Lover. But second, I write as one who knows very well that the world in which we live, and we ourselves as part of that world, must be understood in dynamic, relational, and existentialist fashion. For me this demands that we must have some conceptuality in terms of which our existence may be interpreted and into which Christian faith must be fitted. Bultmann has spoken of the necessity for intelligible 'pre-conceptions' or 'presuppositions' before a biblical student can properly engage in his task of interpretation of the material before him. So likewise I should insist that for any proper theological work there must be a world-view (what I have above called a 'conceptuality') which is defensible, meaningful, and acceptable in the light of our knowledge of ourselves and the world.

This requires me to say here a few words about the particular conceptuality which seems to me demanded today. I can put this in a few brief statements, hoping that the reader will find these useful as he follows the argument in some of the later chapters.

First, ours is a world which is 'in process'; it is marked by change, 'becoming', development – not necessarily for the better, but certainly as a given fact of experience. Second, such a world is one in which the basic constituents are not things or substances which may be located, in a simple fashion, at this point and in this place. Rather, these basic constituents are events or happenings: they are actual occasions which have a subjective side, as 'puffs of experience', and an objective side, as genuinely there in the world and as making up that world for what it is. Third, the past has casual efficacy on the present while the present is the moment in which decisions are made, on the basis of that past and in response to the lure of further possibilities, towards a future which is not yet decided but awaits these decisions to become real. Fourth, every event or occasion in the world is related with, is affected by, and itself affects, other events or occasions. This conceptuality has been worked out most adequately by Alfred North Whitehead, the philosopher from Cambridge in England who ended his days teaching and then living in retirement in Cambridge in the United States, and by his former associate at Harvard University, Charles Hartshorne. Whitehead died in 1947; Hartshorne is still living and writing and is contributing greatly to the further development of this new mode of metaphysical enquiry.

When this conceptuality, which has come to be called 'process thought' (because of the title of Whitehead's famous Gifford lectures *Process and Reality*), is used for theological purposes – as in this book I shall be doing – it has been given the name 'process theology.' I write as one who believes that, of all available world-views in terms of which Christian faith may be stated, this is the most adequate. It is in accord with what we know of ourselves in meditating on our existence and with what we know through observation about the world in which we live. If there be a God, that conceptuality requires that God must be no 'supreme anomaly' or 'exception' to the basic principles necessary to make sense of our existence and our world, but rather 'their chief exemplification' – I am using here Whitehead's own words. Above all, process thought gives us a context in which it may meaningfully be said that persuasion, lure, invitation, and love are basic to the way things go and to the supreme, unsurpassable, adorable, and dependable reality working in things – that is, to God. I hope that what has here been stated so briefly will be made explicit and convincing in the chapters of this book.

I recognize that my conclusions in respect to the significance of talk about 'the future' life will seem to many Christian people to be unsatisfactory, perhaps (to their way of thinking) altogether too minimal, and certainly lacking in providing a 'picture' which resembles much that has commonly been said in religious circles. What is here attempted is a 'demythologizing' of traditional teaching on the subject. In a book published a few years ago I said that one day I should like to engage in just that demythologizing. I have sought to do this in such a way that what is said will be meaningful and helpful to those who are dissatisfied with the conventional portrayal and yet will also be sufficiently loyal to the main drive of Christian faith. For myself I can say that I am utterly convinced, with Mother Julian of Norwich, that in and with God 'all shall be well, all shall be well, and all manner of thing shall be well' – and that includes human existence in and under God.

1

The Fact of Death

In this book I shall try to present a way of understanding our human life 'in God', as I like to phrase it, which will avoid some of the difficulties that many of us find in the conventional talk about 'life after death'. In a way this is an essay in 're-interpretation', but much more than that it is an effort to engage in what seems to me the necessary task of 'de-mythologizing' that position as it is commonly set forth.

But I wish to make clear at the outset that I do not see such 'de-mythologizing' as the entire negation of the perennially Christian conviction that human existence has significance here and now and *also* has a significance beyond this mortal life. It matters to God; hence it is meaningful to speak of the way in which, once we have come to the end of our life in this world, something abides – and that something is of enormous importance and gives dignity to our humanity, both for you and me as particular persons and also for human society in its total reality – a society of which each of us is a member, by virtue of our belonging together in what an Old Testament text beautifully calls 'a bundle of life'.

Before this more positive view can be presented, however, it is essential that we confront honestly and bravely the plain fact that we are going to die. As I shall say, confronting that plain fact does not suggest that we should spend our time in the not very profitable exercise of meditating every day on its reality. But it does require that we should reckon very seriously with our mortality and recognize that this mortality qualifies all that we do and say and think and are.

Perhaps our own age is the first in which much effort has been

1

expended in seeking to avoid any such confrontation, so that it is now generally assumed that while death will inevitably come to each one, the question it poses can be put off to that distant tomorrow. Of course it is true that 'in the midst of life we are in death'; nobody would dare to deny this. But do we really bother much about it?

There can be little doubt that our ancestors, not least in Victorian times, seemed often to be obsessed by the thought of death, both their own and that of other persons. Much fiction included a 'death-bed scene', presented with a sentimental attention to detail; many will remember such scenes in the novels of Charles Dickens, guaranteed to move the reader to tears as each circumstance was described. But quite apart from such exaggerated emphasis, there was certainly a keen awareness of human mortality. This is reflected in hymns written during the nineteenth century, so many of them filled with references to the brevity of life here and now, and usually presenting death as a relief from the pains, sorrows, and miseries of mundane existence. 'Weary of self and laden with my sin, I look to heaven and long to enter in. . . ' So runs one of the most popular of those hymns; and there were many more which in one way or another focused on death as release from *this* life into one which was painted as inevitably a happier state. Of course the thought of hell, or the state opposite to heavenly bliss, was not forgotten either; but fear of such a hell seems to have been a less central note than expectation of 'joy in heaven'.

My present concern, however, is not with an assessment of the significance of the calculus of reward and punishment, so often part of this general acceptance of the fact of death. Rather, it is with the acceptance of death itself. Whatever else may have been wrong about the attitude, at least this can be said: for centuries human beings have been ready to recognize that they were mortal. And to my mind this is a healthier state of mind than a too easy dismissal of the fact of human mortality. The failure of so many of our contemporaries to reckon sufficiently seriously with that mortality is largely responsible for the appalling shock that comes when someone *does* die. Doubtless this also helps to explain the funeral customs of our day, so cynically portrayed in books like *The Loved One* by Evelyn Waugh and *The American Way of Death* by Nancy Mitford.

Funeral directors, undertakers, 'morticians' (as they are called in the United States) may be responsible in large measure for this unrealistic state of affairs. Yet one may assume that such 'professionals' are not so much creating as confirming attitudes already pretty well established. Nor can the clergy of the various Christian and other religious groups be entirely exonerated, for frequently enough they are embarrassed by the fact of death and may even come to the point of saying, 'There is no death' – as a certain minister known to me was in the habit of announcing when he entered the house of a family where death had occurred. An acquaintance of this clergyman remarked that the latter was lying, since plainly there was a corpse somewhere upstairs in the house! The good intention of that minister is not in doubt; but surely the way in which he carried out that intention was nothing more than a confirmation of the common unwillingness to accept honestly the facts of the case.

Contemporary uneasiness about talk of death and the frequent refusal to reckon with it can be interpreted as a welcome, perhaps a necessary, reaction from the morbidity of an earlier age. There is no need to dwell constantly on mortality; healthy recognition of the reality does not require us to spend much of our time in meditating on the subject. To that extent, then, we may well be glad that men and women nowadays are not so engrossed with, even obsessed by, the patent truth that all of us die. Yet this can lead, and in my view has led, to an entirely unrealistic attitude whose only result must be an aggravation of the shock when death does come, threatening each of us and refusing to go away just because we happen not to like facing up to it.

In the course of a pretty long life, I have heard only one sermon which dealt with the subject. I shall never forget the astonishment, not to say horror, with which the congregation heard the preacher, a visiting monk as it happened, begin his sermon by these words: 'Every one of you now sitting in front of me is going to be a corpse; and that, within not too many years.' If the preacher hoped to shock his audience into attention, he certainly succeeded. They listened to what he said after those words; and I suspect that most of them were not able to get over being forced to endure what Henry James, in a very different connection, once styled 'the shock of recognition'. It was good for them to be forced to do this.

3

Now the fact of our death is a writing of *finis* on this our mortal existence. To use an analogy suggested by Professor Charles Hartshorne, it constitutes the last page of our book of life. The story has come to an end; this is its conclusion. It is an inevitable *finis*; and no good purpose is served by denying that such is the case. I should put it in this fashion: not only do we *all* die, which is obvious enough, but *all of us* also dies, which to many may not appear so obvious. We die, body and mind, even 'soul' (if that word is right to use here); and all the talk in the world about 'immortality of the soul' will not deliver us from this kind of finality.

I am well aware of the hangover of vague religiosity which wants to maintain some such 'immortality of the soul', as if there were part of each of us, and the most important part, that did not undergo death. Origins of such a notion go far back in human history, to primitive days when our remote ancestors thought that some special *anima* indwelt human bodies; it was given additional support by the teaching of certain of the Greeks, with their insistence on the soul as entirely distinct from, yet temporarily the tenant of, the body – at its most extreme this expressed itself in the saying *soma sema*, 'the body is the prison-house of the soul'. At death, for those who took this view, the soul or 'spirit' would be released from its captivity in and its bondage to the physical integument which for a time had clothed it; then the soul, taken to be the genuine self, would continue for ever in a state of disembodied existence.

This doctrine is often enough taken to be the Christian way of seeing things. But it is not the biblical view, for what that is worth. In the early days of the Jewish people, death was not seen as such a release; it was taken to be quite definitely final. Some vague and ghostly continuation was granted, in at least some if not all biblical writers; but this continuation was an insignificant and senseless shadow of real life. 'The dead praise not thee, O Lord, neither they that go down to Sheol' – not inappropriately translated in the Authorized Version of the Bible as 'silence', for in Sheol nothing transpires, nothing is heard, nothing is known.

In later years in Jewish history, especially with the Maccabean Wars, belief in a 'resurrection', rather than in natural immortality, began to make its appearance. With their strongly material stress, the Jews naturally thought of such a restoration in terms of a bodily or fleshly 'rising'. Later this was given a more 'spiritual' interpretation, as in some Pharisaic thinking and in Christian times as in such a view as St Paul's in I Corinthians, where there is a 'physical body' and a 'spiritual body'. The latter is not a matter of 'flesh and blood', which (he says) 'cannot inherit the kingdom of heaven'. Rather, it is sort of existence continuous with our life in this world and in the physical body, but not identical with either of these – it is a mode of existence appropriate to 'the heavenly places', although the level or degree of its continuation is to be determined by what has been done 'in the flesh'.

Christian theologians in later ages engaged in the well-nigh impossible task of holding together the 'immortality of the soul' and the 'resurrection of the body'. The synthesis was never worked out in a consistent and logically intelligible fashion, despite the various devices which were employed in the attempt to do this. Just what happened to the 'body' in the interval before the 'end of the days'; just where and what the continuing 'soul' was when separated from that body; just how the two somehow were to be united once again, especially when quite plainly the body had decayed into its several ingredients: these and other questions were never satisfactorily resolved. Hence, as some of us think, the resultant doctrine found in theological text-books under the chapter-heading 'The Last Things' or 'eschatology' is confused and confusing. But there can be little question that over the years the 'immortality' position has been more and more given the primacy, while the 'resurrection' position has been explained away or so modified that its basic intention has been forgotten or lost. To that extent, and in that way, an essentially Greek philosophical, rather than a biblical, teaching has been communicated to the great majority of thoughtful believers.

In later chapters I shall attempt to say positively what, as it seems to me, the 'resurrection' can be taken to affirm. But for the moment I wish only to insist that one of the consequences of the 'immortality' position, for so long presented as essential to Christian belief, has been precisely the tendency to minimize the reality of death and to make it appear blasphemous for anyone to say, as I did in an earlier paragraph, that not only do we all die but that *all of us* also dies. Yet the evidence which we possess, from our much more complete scientific knowledge, would argue that such is indeed the truth.

In that sense, we may agree with Martin Heidegger's oft-quoted talk about human death as being 'the finality' of our existence. We do 'live towards death', as he has noted; and our death marks the end of what we have been up until that moment. Even talk about a possible survival cannot deny that patent fact, once we have understood the total organic, psycho-somatic, nature of our human existence. And here biblical thought, despite its mythological idiom and its scientific inaccuracy, was much more in accordance with common sense, as well as with the actual situation at the time of death. The biblical material stresses the material world, the bodily condition, the time-and-space reality, which we all know and in terms of which we exist as men and women; it does not take flight into some supposedly more 'spiritual' realm where these things are of no importance and where presumably life is lived, at the creaturely level, without any genuinely created order at all.

Death, then, is indeed 'the finality of life'; it is also, as Heidegger equally stressed, 'the finality in life', or (better) 'life in its finality'. That is to say, the fact of our death provides us with something we can readily enough forget or neglect – namely, the insistence that whatever we do, whatever we are, whatever we achieve, have about them the quality of finitude and mortality. Due recognition of our inescapable mortality makes us see also that we do not count for so much in the total cosmic picture as we might like to think. It establishes once and for all our 'expendability', and clearly asserts that, whatever the world as a whole may include or entail, it does not and cannot find its meaning in this mortal existence.

It is not easy for us men and women to accept this. Perhaps the difficulty in accepting it is related to the equal difficulty which is found in accepting the reality of death in its complete and final sense. We do not readily entertain the idea that in many senses we are relatively insignificant in the total scheme of things. Nor do we find attractive the thought that after our death we are likely to be forgotten, no matter how much we may have been valued by others during our lifetime. A few decades and it will be as if we had never been. What is more, the entire history of the human race has an equally limited character. There may be – and one of the purposes of this book is to urge that there is – an abiding significance in our human existence; and it may be that neither we nor anything else is to be utterly forgotten. But before we can come to any such assertion, we must first of all honestly face the mundane reality for what it is. Otherwise we can properly be charged with simply adopting some defence-mechanism which will enable us to evade precisely such uncomfortable truth.

Our ancestors could talk about life here as being greatly important. One Victorian poet wrote that 'life is real, life is earnest'. Perhaps earnestness, in the sense of excessive concern for human rectitude, can be overdone. We ought to be serious about things, but not humourlessly earnest like those tedious characters who often appear in novels of that period. None the less, there is a seriousness about life which most of us acknowledge when we do not permit ourselves to become entirely devoted to the trivia which clutter our days. Their often too dreary attention to the reality of the death which awaited them and everybody else was for those ancestors of ours a way in which they made themselves come to grips with things that really matter. The way in which they did this may not appeal to us; but at least they did find a genuine purpose in their existence, which was made all the more vivid and exacting for them because they understood very well that they faced an end and that after that end had come they could not 'pass this way again'.

When in an earlier book I spoke in this fashion, although concentrating attention on a different subject, and hence mentioned death as 'finality' in Heidegger's two senses, some critics urged that I was falling victim to the gloom associated with the writing and thinking of some of the more atheistic existentialists. But surely this was not true. My purpose then, and also in the present context, is only to stress the fact of mortality, its seriousness, and its capacity to illuminate something of the significance of our present human life in this world. If I had left it there, the criticism might have been valid. But I did *not* leave it there, since I went on to assert that *in God* human finality is in one sense *not* 'the last word'. Later I shall show how it is possible for us to speak in that fashion. But the introduction of the word 'God' at this point makes it necessary for me to say something about what I take to be the Christian conception of deity, drawn from the biblical material as a whole, but above all from the New Testament presentation of what Alfred North Whitehead once called 'the brief Galilean vision'. And mention of Whitehead at once indicates that the perspective or stance from which I approach this discussion of the Christian conception of deity is that of process thought whose 'founding father' Whitehead was.

In this place I need not outline the general position taken by process thought. I have already done this in a number of books, perhaps most plainly in *Process Thought and Christian Faith* (Nisbet and Macmillan 1969) and *The Lure of Divine Love* (T. & T. Clark and Pilgrim Press 1979). Suffice it to say that the conceptuality which I accept – and accept because it seems to do justice to deep analysis of human experience and observation, as well as to the knowledge we now have of the way 'things go' in the world – lays stress on the dynamic 'event' character of that world; on the inter-relationships which exist in what is a societal universe, on the inadequacy of 'substance' thinking to describe such a universe of 'becoming' and 'belonging', on the place of decisions in freedom by the creatures with the consequences which such decisions bring about, and on the central importance of persuasion rather than coercive force as a clue to the 'going' of things in that universe. The conception of deity which I shall now briefly present is not based only on that process conceptuality but on the total impression given by the material contained in the Jewish and Christian scriptures. But I find that what is there communicated is illuminated by, and gives more profound meaning to, the process conceptuality. And I also find that this conceptuality offers a possibility of saying something positive and enriching about the whole business of human existence both in its finitude and in its abiding significance – and this is the case because one of the further emphases in process thought is its recognition of a divine and unsurpassable reality (call this 'God', for that is the traditional term for the supremely worshipful one) which is not only the chief (although not the sole) causative agency in the creation but also the chief receptive and responsive agency in that creation. We shall see presently how helpful this conception can be to us in our consideration of human existence and its worth.

I take it that the Christian conception of God is built upon the prior Jewish understanding of the 'living God' who is active in the creation, who is self-identified with that creation, who shares in its joys and in its anguish, and whose basic intention throughout the creative process is the emergence of finite responsive created agents who with God will work for greater justice, truth, sympathy, righteousness, and goodness. In so doing, these agents will not only fulfil their own possibility; they will also bring enrichment to the divine life – not that God will become any more God than before, but that by virtue of the divine receptivity of what is accomplished in the creation there will be further opportunities for more adequate and complete expression of the divine intention or purpose which is at work in the whole enterprise.

To this earlier Jewish awareness there was given, as a climactic and focal moment in that strand of history, an enactment or expression of the divine Love-in-act: this is what the event we indicate when we say Jesus of Nazareth and the Christ of continuing faith makes available to us. Not that this event is (to use words I have employed in other books) 'the supreme anomaly', as if it contradicted and cancelled what had gone before and what goes on elsewhere. Rather, this event is what I have also styled elsewhere 'the classical instance', in which there is provided a vivid and vitalizing disclosure of the divine Love-in-act and, in consequence of that 'eventful' disclosure, an empowering or enabling of human response which in a very particular way is a re-enactment of the human side in the total event Jesus Christ. The ancient theologians of the Christian tradition had their own idiom for this: they spoke of our becoming *filii in Filio*, 'sons in *the* Son'. For exactly because in that Christ-event there was a climactic and focal expression, the One who is the centre of the event, Jesus himself, was called *the* Son – not to exclude all others from sonship but to interpret *their* sonship in terms of him. And of course 'sonship' is not, in this connection, a male notion; it is inclusive of the human race, male and female, and it is regrettable that we do not seem to have any single word which will put this male-female reality into decently 'non-sexist' phrasing.

In the light of such a 'model of God', as theologians would put it today, there is a possibility of speaking significantly of the enormous value or worth of human existence. This can be done without for a moment negating what I have styled the two 'finalities' about that existence. But it will do one thing which is of very great importance. It will make clear that whatever value or worth our existence may have, it does not reside in ourselves – for we are finite creatures, destined to die, and in that sense expendable. Rather, it resides in the relationship with God which such existence may and does enjoy, whether this is realized or actualized in a vivid manner

9

or is present only as a kind of *Leitmotif* which runs through the whole history of the human race and the personal history of each and every human person as a member of the society of men and women.

For ultimately it is *God* who matters. As I shall try to say in the conclusion and summary of this book, all is for *God's* 'greater glory'. And that glory is no majestic enthronement as almighty ruler and self-exalted monarch, but is the sheer Love-in-act which generously gives, graciously receives, and gladly employs whatever of worth or value has been accomplished in a world where God is faithfully active to create more occasions for more good at more times and in more places.

2

The Loss of Belief in the 'After-life'

If refusal to face squarely the fact of death is found so widely in these days, so also is loss of belief in a continuation of human existence, beyond death, in what used to be called the 'after-life'. It is indeed true that among conventionally-minded church-people and many others there is a vague feeling that when the body dies the 'soul' goes on. But that feeling is *very* vague, or so I have come to think when I have considered the attitude of many of my friends and acquaintances. The strong conviction which seems to have been found in an older generation, especially among those who would have styled themselves 'believers', is nowadays very infrequent. Once death has occurred, that is taken to be in truth the *end*.

Now we have here a rather contradictory state of affairs. In the first place, thought about death is avoided so far as possible. The reality of it, the sheer fact of it, does not figure prominently in most people's minds. But in the second place, once the inevitable has taken place, there is nothing more to be said. Death, however much its coming has been forgotten or minimized, has now occurred. And since it *has* occurred, there is nothing further to be thought. For what my own opinion is worth, I should say that even among those who are regular church-going people and who would be classified as Christian men and women, there is no very certain conviction about life 'after death'. Such people may accept, with the top of their minds, what they have been led to think is Christian teaching on the subject, but this teaching is not deeply rooted nor profoundly felt. Rather, it cuts little if any ice, as one might put it.

I am not denying for a moment the presence, especially in older people, of some genuine belief in the 'after-life'. I am only saying

11

that for many, if not most, of them it is not a deep conviction which makes a genuine difference in their basic attitude towards existence. I should also say that with younger people, more particularly those who have been reasonably well educated, the belief itself appears to have faded away. Why is this so? What has happened to produce such a different view from the one that is an earlier age was prevalent – certainly with church-people and often enough, although in an attenuated sense, with those who seemed to have no settled religious beliefs?

There are probably many reasons, to be sure. I do not myself agree with the notion found in some circles that it is all part of what is regarded as the God-less materialism of our age. In fact, of course, there *is* such materialism around us, if by this we mean an emphasis on the things of here-and-now, as well as a striving for the comforts and convenience of life without too much, if any, concern for what used to be called 'spiritual valuves'. There can be little doubt that in civilized societies at the present time the stress is put on living as well as one can in the present moment or for a fairly short future. But the loss of a clearly defined belief in an 'after-life' is not adequately explained by this patent fact. There are other factors, some of which should now be mentioned.

For one thing, the old notion of a life after death which will provide some compensation for evils endured in this present existence does not make much sense. This kind of thought, which at its worst was found in the parody popularized decades ago that 'there'll be pie in the sky, when you die' as a compensation for injustice today, is hardly attractive to men and women who insist that justice is to be done *now*. Even in its more sophisticated guise, such as the argument of Immanuel Kant that life in heaven is to be a due adjustment of affairs after the obvious evil known and experienced in mundane life, there is for many people little meaning. And with this has gone also the old idea that what might be called 'the rewards and punishment syndrome' demands that there should be a post-mortem existence for these rewards and punishments to take place. 'The fear of hell' does not play any significant part in the thinking of most of our contemporaries; neither does contemplation of the 'joy of heaven'.

One reason here, I believe, is that the somewhat crude way in which the rewards and punishment motif was presented seems nothing short of ridiculous – and in any event, not very appealing, even when 'heaven' is talked about. Hell-fires and eternal (or unending) suffering was at one time regarded as a deterrent from wrong-doing. But the fires of hell seem to have been quenched; or at least they do not figure very largely in contemporary thinking, nor, for that matter, in contemporary preaching and teaching. On the other hand, the picture of heaven as a kind of featureless bliss or (worse) a graphic but somewhat physically represented state of existence whose dominant characteristic is 'doing nothing' hardly arouses much enthusiasm. The usual stress upon 'rest eternal' is hardly likely to make much appeal to men and women who have been convinced that life, as they know and value it, entails activity and 'doing things'. This kind of picture seems to contradict all that such people feel to be worthwhile. Maybe some sort of 'rest' would be welcomed for a short time, after the incessant 'busy-ness' of our mortal days; but in the long run, it would be tedious and unattractive.

Another factor which has tended to make talk about the 'after-life' less than appealing may be found in the feeling that much of that talk about it is highly self-centred – a matter of 'glory for me'. Nobody could argue that we are living in an age when there is a universal awareness of societal relationships as constitutive of human existence. Certainly the fact of our social belonging cannot be denied. The truth that 'no man is an island unto itself' is patent enough. But very many people seem to want to live as if it were not such a truth. Yet on the other hand, men and women nowadays are uncomfortable with any position which would be so *totally* individualistic that the place of such social belonging is utterly neglected. They feel that they *ought* to consider their fellows; and when they are thinking seriously about life they know that 'rugged individualism' is both wicked and self-defeating. If they are at all sensitive, the presentation of the Christian gospel as a purely individual 'salvation' appears to be outrageous. I say this because no matter how successful, in an obvious way, such preaching may be, its principal value is that 'the old-time religion' (thus conceived and proclaimed) provides for insecure and uncertain men and women an authority to which they may bow and thus be delivered, as they think, from too much victimization by the 'changes and chances of this mortal life'. I doubt if such a presentation of the Christian

13

gospel is other than a palliative for those who are insecure, as well as offering a sort of reassurance to people who have been induced (often by quite dubious techniques) to feel enormously guilty about themselves. For the thoughtful person the idea of 'glory for me', or a strictly individualistic salvation, is not highly attractive. Such a person recognizes, albeit not too clearly, that whatever salvation is possible and whatever 'glory' is worth having, it *must* be inclusive of and attentive to the rest of the human race.

If something like this is the case, then a highly individualistic and self-centred interest in and desire for life beyond death will not make much sense. It would be unfair as well as unkind to say that a good deal of the older yearning for that post-mortem existence, usually expressed in talk about immortality, was nothing but self-ishness. Often enough it was a consequence of the profound import-ance of the love which had dignified and enriched life here and now. It would have been unthinkable that such love, shared between men and women as the best thing in their experience, was to be utterly extinguished. Shared love at its best seems to have a certain eternal quality; nothing can destroy it. And one way in which this experienced reality can be guaranteed for what it is would be by affirming that when this life is ended the loving rela-tionships will somehow be continued and given fuller and finer expression. The question is whether the usual talk of immortality is a possible or even desirable way of assuring the validity of such a conviction about love and its meaning. Here many people hesitate, for they can make little sense of the conventional pictures, such as are found in much hymnody and in many of the devotions which we have inherited from our Christian past. If the assurance is real, there must be a better way of interpreting it – or so they would feel.

As I shall urge in the sequel, the assurance is indeed genuine enough; love *is* stronger than death. We need desperately to find a way of saying this which will be able to stand up to criticism, above all a way which will be congruous with the basic Christian affirmation that God is both central in the universe and is best described as 'the Love that will not let us – or anyone or anything – go. . .' It is God who alone can give enduring value and worth to the things that we, in our tiny way and with our limited finite understanding, also find of worth and value. Or, to put it otherwise and in a manner which must be developed as we proceed in our discussion, it is God who matters supremely. The Jewish-Christian tradition at its best and when most true to its deepest insight is incurably and unfailingly theocentric: 'God-centred'.

I have said that the charge of excessive secularistic materialism, frequently made against modern people, is not accurate. What *is* correct, however, is the concern which they show for what goes on 'in the body'. They are not prepared to agree with the medieval hymn-writer who said that 'the times are very evil' – if by those words it is being said that the world itself, the things of this world, the experiences known in this world, are in and of themselves bad. Of course if that writer intended something else, as he may well have done, namely that the 'times', in the sense of the particular segment of history in which he lived, were indeed 'evil' and were marked by wickedness, with a collapse of standards and the denial of all that is of abiding significance; if he intended that, there may well have been much truth in his statement. If, however, his line of thought reflected the Manichean rejection of this world as such, of things made of matter and of all that is thus materially embodied, no responsible Catholic or Protestant Christian thinker could agree. In this respect, contemporary 'materialism' (if that is the right word here) is much *more* in accordance with the biblical presentation, in which God does not deny or negate the creation but affirms it, identifies himself with it, and acts within it. So far as specifically Christian faith is in the picture, the traditional doctrine of the 'incarnation of God' in this world would be a further and decisive statement of the essential goodness of the material creation, including the human body and its workings – since for that faith God was 'enfleshed' in a human body, made up as it is of the stuff of the material world. We may not be happy with the particular fashion in which this conviction was expressed in the several classical formulations; we may seek for and hope to find a way of stating this conviction which does not depend upon the philosophy of ancient Greek thinkers. Yet the conviction itself stands firm, if we intend to be responsible Christians whose faith is in continuity with that of the so-called 'ages of faith'.

In those days, not least in the thinking of men like St Thomas Aquinas, the material world was regarded as a good thing, although wrongdoing of various sorts had distorted and perverted it in the forms in which actually we experience it. Grace, or the divine good-

15

will and the divine activity, did not 'destroy nature but perfected it'. So the Angelic Doctor vigorously affirmed. And when he was thinking about human existence itself, he was intent upon saying that a whole human person was compounded of body as well as of soul; in the end, he said, the two would be reunited after the separation which death had brought about. Here, of course, he was thinking in terms of the typical philosophical understanding of his day: soul and body were taken to be distinct but also mutually involved in human existence. He was accepting the immortality of the soul; but he was also urging that a mere soul, without a body of some kind, did not constitute the genuine and complete human person. The soul was for him the *form* of the body; the body the *matter* of the soul. The two belonged together in what Aristotelian thought styled the hylo-morphic nature of 'manhood'. Although his way of working this out may not appeal to us, with our quite different scientific knowledge, and our own philosophical idiom, the point here is that Aquinas, like the other theologians of the great Christian tradition, was no 'spiritualist', denying or minimizing the material world and the physical body and their ways of working. In this sense that tradition was getting at what in our own day we should call the 'psychosomatic' constitution of human being. Alas, many of those who would style themselves devout Christians are in fact believers in the Manichean rejection of the world as not only temporal and in the obvious sense ephemeral but also as evil and without spiritual worth. St Thomas fought that position with all his intellectual and religious power. Such people need to be taught the truth which a modern poet stated:

How can we love thee, holy hidden Being,
If we love not the world which thou hast made. . .

There is still another point to be stressed. One element in our contemporary thinking, which has helped to make talk of the 'after-life' appear meaningless, is the increasing recognition that there is no such thing as a 'substantial self'. Even those who are not informed about contemporary psychological analysis of human experience may very well feel that it is not adequate to describe that experience as if we were speaking about some persistent 'I', *to* which things happened; a self which did things that were, so to say, merely adjectival to the substantival 'I'. Those who feel this way believe that none of us is like a clothes-line upon which the

16

Monday washing is hung. In that picture, the clothes-line is the *real* self, the *genuine* identity of the 'I', and the various articles hung on the line for drying are the particular moments or occasions of human experience. It would be perfectly possible, in that case, to remove the articles of clothing, while the clothes-line would still remain intact. The men and women who today have somehow glimpsed what a good deal of psychological analysis confirms, believe that the line and the clothes are mutually related; so that on the one hand there is no sense in talking of the line without the clothes, while without the line – that is, without *some* significant meaning in human selfhood or identical 'I'-ness – the experiences represented by the articles hung on the line would be a collection of happenings that have no claim to significance and are only chance moments without worth.

If something like this is the fact, it is then easy to see why a 'self', totally detached from its experiences, is hardly worth preservation. What am I, what are you, what is anybody, without the things we have said and done, the things that have been said to us and done with and for us? The answer would seem to be, 'Nothing at all; or at least, nothing worth bothering about.'

The importance of these considerations will emerge in the next chapter, when we shall have to discuss human existence as a matter of both body and mind. My point at the moment is only to suggest that one of the reasons for the loss of belief in a life after death is precisely the growing acceptance of just such a portrayal of what each one of us really *is*. But the other factors to which I have referred are equally operative; and there may be still more about which we have not spoken. The truth is, however, that for whatever reasons, the strong conviction of post-mortem human existence in any subjective and self-conscious sense does not mark today the thinking of vast numbers of our fellow men and women.

In this respect, they are not too different from the Old Testament worthies to whom I have referred in another context. One of my former students, after a long and detailed study of the evidence found in the Hebrew Scriptures, has concluded that for the greater part of their history the Jewish people had no certain conviction about a post-mortem continuation of human beings. He has said that more and more he is impressed by the way in which their vivid and vital faith in God was maintained in spite of all sorts of difficulties, including their own suffering and defeats. Perhaps naively, they were sure that in *this* life there would be an overturning of evil, with God as the principal agent in that overturning. None the less, they did not ask nor did they assume that there would be some compensation after their death for that which they had experienced and undergone. My friend went on to say that it seemed to him that in a way this long Jewish theocentrism, without belief in 'immortality' as such, was a nobler and grander kind of faith than the much more man-centred position of later ages. Even today, he remarked, Jewish faith seems to be less focused on what is likely to happen to *us* than upon what *God is doing in the world*. Whatever one may think of this, certainly it cannot be doubted that it is possible for devout people, firm believers in the reality of God and in God's care for those who are his children, to put little, if any, stress upon an 'after-life'.

I do not wish to give the impression, however, that what used to be believed in respect to existence after death is in my view entirely without value. The 'de-mythologizing' of this belief is necessary; but it equally important for us to respect, as we must also come to recognize, the probability of some genuine insight which got itself stated in a set of ideas which nowadays seem to carry little weight for vast numbers of our human comrades. In other words, there are positive things which must be said, quite as much as there are negative things. It is obvious that at the very time when life beyond death is no longer a matter of vital importance, there is an increasing emphasis on the worth of human personality. Some may say that this emphasis lacks any substantial support, such as (to their mind) the older belief could provide. It is easy to dismiss the contemporary insistence on such personal worth as being without foundation, or as nothing more than a dim remembrance of the day when it might have been based on firm assurance about subjective immortality. But this, I believe, is both wrong-headed and short-sighted.

The *real* grounding for the emphasis on the worth of persons is of another sort. It rests upon an inchoate, frequently dimly understood, sense that life in itself is valuable, that human life is especially valuable, and that somehow the very grain of the universe is on its side. Schubert Ogden and others have written compellingly on the way in which, deep down in human experience, there is an assumption (however unconscious this may be, most of the time) that 'no

18

matter what the content of our choices may be, whether for this course of action or for that, we can make them at all only because of our invincible faith that they somehow make a difference which no turn of events has the power to annul' (*The Reality of God*, SCM Press 1967, p. 36). Ogden goes on to speak of the way in which modern men and women are deeply convinced that 'it is our own secular decisions and finite processes of creative becoming which are the very stuff of the "really real" and so themselves somehow of permanent significance' (ibid., p. 64).

Now such a position requires a doctrine of God which need not be formally defined and stated, but which deeper analysis can show to be implicitly present. The doctrine of God may be different in many respects from that which hitherto has been urged as the only possible Christian teaching. Nevertheless, it may be – and I agree with Ogden that it is – more than a *theory*; indeed, it may be, and I am convinced that it is, a much more defensible understanding than the traditionally accepted one. More must be said about this, although in the opening chapter I have already mentioned it. Let me end this chapter with a further quotation from Ogden's important book:

'At the beginning and end of all our ways is One in whose steadfast will and purpose there is indeed no shadow of turning and in whom all our confidences have their unshakable foundation. . . In his inmost actuality he is "pure unbounded love", pure personal relation to others, who has no other cause than the ever more abundant life of the creatures of his love. Far from being something to which even the greatest of our accomplishments is worth nothing at all, he is the One who makes even the least of things to be of infinite worth by giving it a share in his own infinite and all-encompassing life. He is, in fact, just that "enduring remembrance", except for which our perishing lives as creatures would indeed be vanity and a striving after wind. . . [Such a theism] enables us at last really to understand our confidence that the whole of our life is unconditionally worth while' (ibid., p. 142).

3

Human Existence in Body and Mind

Towards the end of the last chapter, I spoke of the mistake, so frequent in the past, of looking at human existence in terms of a substantial self to which experiences happened or by which experiences are had. Certainly it has commonly been thought that each of us is an 'I' whose existence is in no significant sense dependent upon such experiences. I insisted that there *is* a genuine personal identity; but it has been assumed that this identity is made possible by the fact that there is just this kind of substantial self. It is that view which (as it is thought) makes possible and seems to lend probability to the notion that the self, so understood, can continue to exist even when there is no body and when there are no further experiences of a sort appropriate to bodily life.

For myself, it is clear that such a picture of selfhood cannot stand up to criticism. That I feel myself to be an 'I' and that I act in terms which entail a continuity of that 'I' with what has gone before and what will follow after, is an unquestionable fact. What is more, there can be no denying the human sense of accountability for what has been done by this 'I'. But that need not require us to think that there is a body-mind dichotomy, with the mind as a substantial entity that can be separated from the body, and when thus separated continue to 'be' without any real difficulty. William James showed, years ago, that a quite different account can very well be given; and James was only one of the many psychologists who have denied that there is valid evidence for the reality of a substantial self which is independent not only of the body but also of happenings to the body.

There is a further consideration. If we adopt the analysis of human existence which is urged by Whitehead and other process thinkers – an analysis which leads to generalizations that are found to fit in with much else in our observation of the world – then it is absurd to talk in such substantial terms. For in such an analysis, what is disclosed is that we are in truth a certain direction or routing of events which, because of a persisting memory of what has occurred along it, and because there has emerged (at some point in the evolutionary development so far as our own species is concerned) an awareness which includes both consciousness and self-consciousness, may meaningfully be given a specific identity. That I am I and that you are you rests upon the evident truth that the series of occurrences which have been mine, and those which have been yours, are not identical. My past – that is, the series of experiences which take place along *my* routing – is not the same as yours. The enormous variety of such happenings, given a particular focus in this or in that routing, means that what has appeared as my identity will have characteristics which differ from yours.

Nor is it only a matter of the routing in the past. There is also the fact of decisions made in the tiny instant of choice. On the basis of past experience, one routing (now come to awareness) selects one set of possibilities, while another routing selects another set. The lures or attractions, the invitations or potentialities, of one are not the same as those of the other. The aims which are in view, as each conscious routing makes its selection, are also different one from the other. Such aims are to a considerable degree dependent upon the accomplished past; they are also suggested possibilities as to ways in which fulfilment or satisfaction may be obtained in a further advance. There are marked differences in these aims, although all of them are ways in which there can be the achievement of some significant degree of realization of genuine possibilities which opportunity offers.

Of course what we call 'common sense' does not immediately see the concrete situation for what it is. We are so accustomed to thinking in other ways, thanks to centuries of philosophical and religious teaching, that we are very ready to talk about substantial selfhood. More than that, we all feel deeply our own identity; and it appears to us that the only way in which that feeling can be given validity is by our assuming just such a substantial self. But what is discovered to us in the analysis of experience may quite adequately be interpreted in another way; and it is that other way that I have proposed.

When I try to understand my experience of being human, I find that perhaps the most prominent feature is my memory. There is the conscious memory, standing as it were very much in the forefront of human awareness. There is a kind of memory which is deep in those hidden areas to which the depth psychologists refer when they talk of the 'sub-conscious'. There is also a memory which is grounded in my bodily existence – a visceral memory, as we might call it. This memory is of a past which has brought me to where now I stand; in doing that, it has been causally effective. What holds all this together is the way in which the things remembered are so related that there is a single direction taken by each of them, one characteristic of myself and another characteristic of you. There is a reproduction, in that continuing succession, of specific patterning; there is a dominant occasion, to use Whiteheadian language, which transmits its own particular quality from moment to moment. Through the various sequential events it 'presides' over the routing which is mine or which is yours.

By virtue of a complicated arrangement of cells in the brain, there is at the human level emergent a mental state marked by what I have styled awareness. At the animal level this may be only a vague awareness of that which is distinct from the experiencing subject, without the additional vivid quality known in human life. That additional quality is the awareness of the self *as aware*; it is '*self*-consciousness'. But notice that this kind of awareness is always of the self as experience. It is impossible for me to know any selfhood apart from experience; I cannot abstract, so to say, from my experience and come to an awareness of some non-experiential existence. The awareness of one's selfhood and the fact of one's experience go together. This depends upon there being a brain, an arrangement of cells in a particular part of the body which by reason of its peculiar coordination makes the given routing able to 'know' in a distinctively human manner – quite different from, although certainly continuous with, the sort of 'knowing' that is possible for the higher grades of animal life.

Granted all this, we may now meaningfully proceed to what might be called a phenomenology of human existence in its body-mind complex. But before that, it is worth saying that the kind of

22

mind-body situation which we have been considering provides a strong case against the notion of some continuation after death of the conscious self that had existed before death. The usual line is that precisely because mind and body – or, if you will, 'soul' in its conventional sense and material body; or *res cogitans* and *res extensa* in Descartes' philosophical treatment – are not only entirely distinct one from the other but are also separable one from the other, there can be no denying the possibility, even the strong probability, that when the latter has died the former goes on. The old argument about the violin, as a material thing, and the tune, as a 'spiritual' one, is a pretty fair indication of the position adopted. The instrument may perish but the tune survives – and, as it is often argued by those who would attempt to bring 'immortality of the soul' and some residual meaning of 'resurrection' together into a single conception, that tune might very well be played on another instrument if one does not accept the idea that tunes can exist, so to say, without any expression through some instrumentality. What is not usually recognized is that even if some such persistence of the mind or soul does take place, there is no reason for thinking that this will be an enduring fact. Perhaps C. D. Broad's speculation, in one or two of his writings, may be more probable; like the tune, the 'soul' lingers on for a while; but after a time its existence also comes to an end. Of course the basic difficulty here is that talk of the sort I have just been sketching fails to see that only *in God* (who is himself enduring or everlasting) can any genuinely significant existence, of whatever sort, be guaranteed.

To return, however, to the phenomenology of human existence, we may begin simply by reasserting what so far in this chapter has been stated again and again – namely, that human existence is a body-mind or mind-body complex; and that the two go together in a most intimate and interdependent fashion. A good deal of so-called 'religious' discussion has been conducted on altogether too highly spiritual a plane, as if human beings were really nothing but angels who for the time being happened to be resident in a physical abode. Such a view would be more appropriate for proponents of ancient gnostic theories, come alive again in our day, than for those who profess a biblical basis for their religion. None the less, much that has been taught and preached in the Christian churches has resembled this heretical theorizing. Yet we all know that the body and the mind (or soul) are both so much ourselves that we can say with the poet that it is hard to tell 'whether soul helps body more than body soul'. Our present knowledge of the psychosomatic nature of much human illness, to give but one example, is clear proof that such is indeed the case.

But if an adequate phenomenology of human existence begins with due acceptance of our mind-body condition, it must go on to speak of the dynamic quality which we all know very well in our experience. We are not finished articles; we are moving, developing, changing, growing – this may be for good or for bad, since there seems no reason to assure an inevitable progression in a favourable direction; but whether for good or bad, there is no denying the dynamism of our existence. This, of course, is in accordance with our earlier comments about direction or routing; and any accurate portrayal of human existence is to be found, not in some static cross-section at this or that moment, but rather in the movement which that existence is taking from the past, through the present, towards the future. We are 'on the go'; there is no stopping-place at which it would be possible to say, 'this given moment exhausts what we are'. Only at our death would any such statement have meaning; and when it did, the meaning would be that of a corpse, something indeed finished because 'done for'.

At each point along the routing, we build upon the inherited or acquired past achievements which have their causal influence upon us. In every present moment we are 'aiming' – at the human level with a genuine degree of conscious awareness – at a future. The present is 'specious', as academics would put it; it is the instant which joins a remembered past and an anticipated future, but in and of itself it cannot be said to provide any fixed stance. 'The process *is* the actuality', as Whitehead once put it; to be at all is to become; thus our existence is in our becoming.

At the same time, we are societal creatures in a societal universe. If we are becoming, we are also *belonging*. In the most evident sense, we belong with our fellows in the total human enterprise. Neighbours and friends, family and associates, the human race of which we are part; all these, as any profound understanding of our humanity makes clear enough, are contributory to our own becoming and we on our side make a similar contribution to them. If John Donne was correct in his famous saying that 'no man is an island

24

entire unto itself', then we can only have genuine existence when we are aware of what is thus an inescapable truth about us. This does not require our being vividly conscious, at every moment, of our situation of belonging. What it does demand is that we shall live as what we are, that is, as those who participate in the total human situation and thus live not only with, but from and by and for, others.

This dependence upon other humans does not, however, exhaust the reality of such belonging. We are also dependent on the fact of our being part of, as we have biologically emerged from, the natural order and all that this implies. The too frequent total concentration upon the human, to the exclusion of due recognition and acceptance of the non-human environment, is one of the sad consequences of our altogether overly 'man-centred' way of seeing things. Not only for food and shelter, for clothing and all else that provides us with what used to be styled 'the comforts and conveniences of life', but also for the sheer fact of our existence at all, we cannot escape from this natural order which surrounds us and of which, indeed, we are from one point of view simply a complicated instance. Thus we need constantly to follow Ezra Pound's admonition to 'put down our vanity', a vanity which foolishly pretends that we and we only are the important entities in the cosmos. St Francis of Assisi, with his grateful delight in 'brother sun' and 'sister moon' and all other creatures, animate and inanimate, spoke for the truly human attitude. He understood, doubtless in a naive fashion, that when we are most keenly aware of our own humanity we are aware also of our brotherly-sisterly relationship with everything else. Furthermore, it is very hard to draw a precise and definite line of demarcation between our own bodily existence and that of the world around us. The energies which constitute us are, so to say, passing in and out of our most intimate environment and are effecting and affecting changes in all that surrounds us.

A continued analysis of our existence discloses also that while we are indeed 'minds', in that we have some degree of rationality and are able to engage in thought, in order to understand much about the world and about our own existence and to project plans and work towards goals which will bring us towards actualization of potentiality, we are also to a very large extent creatures of feeling. By this I do not refer merely to the physical sensitivity given through touch, sight, hearing, smell, taste, etc. I refer also to the human experience of aesthetic appreciation, along with our capacity for evaluating, enjoying, suffering, and in other ways becoming sensitively aware of what is both within us and around us. Much Western philosophy has been inadequate at this point. One of the helpful aspects of increasing knowledge of Eastern and other non-European cultures – in India, China, Japan, and the like, as well as African and more primitive modes of experience – has been the forcing upon us, in our all too rational and moral Western world, of exactly this different perspective. The Greek inheritance, through philosophers like Plato and Aristotle, has often been blamed for our excessive rational-moral focus. That is not entirely just, however, since some of the Greeks were far from being thus almost exclusively concentrated on the rational and the moral. In that superb study of Greek throught among the ordinary people of the land, Erwin Rohde's book *Psyche* (Kegan Paul 1920), there is clear indication of this stress on what I might call, following William James, 'feeling-tones' or the more widely and deeply aesthetic mode of awareness.

The point is that human beings are 'poets', although usually they do not grasp this truth about themselves. They are poets in their total existence because they feel more deeply, and experience more truly than is often recognized, aspects of the world which are not easily put into logical formulae and which do not fit into the moral codification that superficially appears to be their main interest. When Tennyson writes in *In Memoriam* of the way in which somebody can say, 'I have *felt*', he is not describing a distortion of human understanding nor is he commending sheer irrationality. Rather, he is stating the imaginative quality which is a natural accompaniment of all human experience. Even when we have done all in our power to destroy such imagination and turn everything into dull prose, men and women still can and do manifest that they are able to dream, to delight in beauty, to appreciate and enjoy.

This brings us to a consideration of the freedom which our analysis also reveals as integral to human existence. Of course that freedom is not unlimited. We belong in a certain place and we live at a certain time; we are 'conditioned' by many factors which are unavoidable if we are indeed creatures of a time-and-space world. Furthermore, our inheritance from the past, with its causal efficacy upon us, establishes limits and restricts us in our choices. Yet the fact of our freedom, with its own causative quality, is not to be denied. A totally deterministic theory contradicts our clearly known sense of freedom. One might say that such a theory is in itself a case of self-contradiction, for nothing could be more absurdly self-contradictory than for a person to expend much effort in an attempt to convince others that they are not really open to conviction because they are determined, by that which is not themselves, to think, to believe, and to act as they do!

We are aware, then, of some genuine although not unlimited freedom of decision, so that we can be said to be (in at least some senses) causes of our selfhood (*causa sui*, as the Latin saying goes). And such decisions have their consequences. They make things happen; they bring about results which otherwise would not have occurred. If this be true, as most obviously it is, there is also a human accountability for what takes place. Here, too, analysis of the experience which we all know provides confirmation. However much we may try to blame somebody or something else – our human associates, our human situation, our past experience, and the like – the human response when most perceptive is to say that '*I* am accountable'. Other considerations may enter in, to be sure; but in the last resort most of us would affirm such a genuine responsibility and it is a mark of our existence, when at its most human, to accept this whether we do it willingly or unwillingly.

There is also another point to remember. Human existence is experienced by us in sexual terms. By this I mean that deep in our awareness is a recognition both of the drive for relationships with others and of the capacity to express this drive in specific actions. The human race is male and female, since obviously its members are equipped with the physical characteristics of gender, some of the female sort, others of the male. At the same time, there is a sense in which the usual portrayal of sexual 'roles' is a matter of social inheritance and social pressures. Gentleness is not exclusively feminine, nor self-assertion exclusively masculine. There is a sexual 'scale', as the Kinsey Reports have shown. Each of us belongs somewhere on that scale, but those who are predominantly male may also possess female qualities, while those who are predominantly female may have male characteristics. Anatomically we are men *or* women; but that is not the whole story. One of the tragedies

27

of our culture has been a too complete separation of maleness and femaleness.

Finally, and with its physiological grounding in that sexuality which is integral to human existence, there is the drive towards, and the capacity for, loving. Underneath all that is on the surface of their lives humans wish to live in love; and without such love their existence is truncated and damaged. It is the poets and artists, the seers and the saints, who have best stated this. Such men and women have understood that 'the strongest power in the world is that of love itself, which does not work by force to achieve its highest purpose or win its greatest victories'. These are words spoken by one of the world's greatest living biochemists, Dr Joseph Needham, in the course of a sermon preached before the University of Oxford in May 1977, and reproduced in the magazine *Theology* for July 1978. Dr Needham went on to say that 'love is vulnerable, inevitably doomed to suffering'; it is aware of rejection, unkindness, cruelty, evanescence, and coldness in the response often made to it. Yet, he insists, such love is 'the truth about human relationships' and it is 'the life which all men and women must lead if the patterns of the Tao [here Needham is using the Chinese notion of the 'way of the universe'] are to be fulfilled on earth'.

In this chapter I have attempted to present an understanding of our human existence which is true to the facts, so far as we know them, which makes sense of and gives sense to our experience, and which indicates what is meant when we speak, as we do, of the worth and value in our lives. The one thing that I have not so far stressed, and I end this chapter by stressing it, is that any profound analysis of our humanity demonstrates all too plainly that we are defective creatures. Honesty compels us to recognize that we seek our own will and way, we try to stop the creative advance when it seems to go against our fond desires, we are content to remain in backwaters and deviate into side-channels, we love either imperfectly or in the wrong ways, we wish to over-ride and control others of our kind, we spoil the environment and refuse our proper human stewardship of the natural order. In other words, we are constantly in danger of being too cheerfully optimistic about ourselves and we need to be reminded again and again that such optimism is foolishly unrealistic. But that does not mean that we must become utterly pessimistic about human existence. Certainly for Christian faith such a pessimism would be disloyal to the conviction that behind, through, and in all our existence there is a relationship with a Love which is enduring, undefeated and indefeasible, faithful in its caring and able to preserve in its own unsurpassable life all that has been worthily achieved in the created order – including all that has been worthily achieved by us humans.

4

Relationship with God

In the conclusion of the last chapter I spoke of a relationship with God which gave to our human existence its value and worth. But I did not insist that this relationship should always be of a explicitly conscious variety. There can very well be a relationship which is not thus known but which nevertheless is constant and inescapable. One of the mistakes in much religious discussion is the insistence that what is usually called 'religious experience' must be a matter of just such conscious awareness, whereas a more satisfactory and defensible view would hold that those moments of awareness, in the specific sense of conscious knowledge of what is taking place, are best interpreted as the 'peak experiences' (to use Abraham Maslow's phrase) for a persistent fact of which, for the most part, we are not keenly conscious but which continues as a sort of *Leitmotif* through the whole of our human existence.

When in the Old Testament (and in the New Testament, too, for that matter) it is said that man *is* or *possesses* 'spirit', it is necessary to enquire just what is being affirmed. It is evident that the use of the term 'spirit' by the ancient Jews was a hypostatizing of something that was very real in their experience. They indicated this reality by saying that a *thing* (as one might put it) known as the spirit was present in human beings; they also spoke of God as being or having such a 'thing'. But what were they really getting at, when they spoke in this fashion? I believe that their use of the idea of 'spirit' or 'a spirit' was the way in which they sought to express the capacity for relationship. Thus to talk about 'the spirit of man' was to say that human existence is not only a matter of mind and body, as we have represented this in our previous discussion, but is also

30

a matter of relationship, in which there is an openness to, and a sharing in, the life of others. To speak of man's spirit, the *human* spirit, is to assert that between and among humans there is a capacity for participation or mutuality. To speak of *God's* Spirit is to assert that in God too there is a characteristic capacity of being open to and entering into contact with others – in this case, with human existence and with the given instances of created men and women whom God delights to know and with whom he enters into communion. There is a mutuality of concern and care, a continuing relationship sustained on both sides, between God and his creatures. That contact may be of varying degrees of intensity and directness; it may be vivid and clear, or it may be dim and vague. But whatever may be its intensity or directness it is always there. On God's side, it is the divine acceptance of, receptivity to, and response made towards the creature. On the human side, it is the always potential and often the actually realized sense of dependence upon the divine reality that sustains and (as traditional language would phrase it) 'saves' such existence from triviality, meaninglessness, and extinction.

In one way or another, the great world religions have grasped this truth. They have talked about it in most diverse fashion, but they have all been intent upon making it a basic factor in the interpretation of the lives of men and women, whoever they may be, wherever they may live, and whatever idiom they may have found useful or helpful in putting into some sort of language this persistent fact in the total experience of members of the human race. In the tradition which we of the Jewish-Christian inheritance know best, the way in which this abiding factor is presented is through talk in terms of 'spirit', human and divine. The relationship of the finite creature with the supremely worshipful and unsurpassable deity is being affirmed; and along with it there is also affirmed the possibility of its becoming on occasion a matter of conscious knowledge on the part of the human, as it is always a present reality in the very nature of God himself.

That relationship is all of a piece, in one sense. God does not alter in his faithful care for his creatures; he is always and everywhere the supreme Love which moves towards, with, and in the creation. On the other hand, the events in the historical order make their contribution to God and hence make available to God different ways in which the relationship may be given expression. However badly the older theology may have phrased it, the abiding truth is that what goes on in the world must matter to God; it must also have its real affect in the way in which the divine-human relationship is maintained, extended, and (dare I say?) enriched. This is the truth hidden in the talk about God's being 'reconciled to us'. Theologians who have quite properly protested against the notion that God was such that he needed to be made friendly and available to his creatures by reason of some event (in this case the death of Christ) which opened up for him this possibility, have failed to see that in this inadequate and often misleading way of speaking, there was an insight of which they should have taken due account. That insight is nothing other than the understanding that while in one sense God is indeed unalterable in his faithfulness, his love, and his welcome to his human children, in another sense the opportunities offered to him to express just such an attitude depend to a very considerable degree upon the way in which what has taken place in the world provides for God precisely such an opening on the human side; and it is used by him to deepen his relationship and thereby enrich both himself and the life of those children.

Part of our difficulty is to be found in the unfortunate notion that the divine is not susceptible of *any* kind of change. Even when it is properly affirmed that God is always and everywhere himself, in his basic nature as Love-in-act, and hence that there is a sense in which God is immutable and unalterable, it needs also to be said that in the divine adaptation to and self-disclosure in the world, there are many different ways in which this may and does take place. And the different ways are relative to that which has happened in the created order – that is, once we grant that what occurs in that order is genuinely significant and has its inevitable consequences. A portrayal of God which would see him as in *no* sense thus affected would be alien to the general biblical picture, and would reduce human activity to a meaningless and irrelevant series of events. In the conceptuality which we are here accepting, such a position is impossible; while in the biblical perspective it is senseless and absurd. The God of Israel is one whose 'ear is open' to the prayers of his people and whose response to their prayers, as also to their acts, is determined by the sort and quality of their human and historical situation. This biblical understanding fits in with and

32

confirms the insight of a process conceptuality in which God is influenced by the creation, although whatever happens in that creation cannot cause him to deny or contradict his essential character as Love.

In the religious tradition which we inherit, it is a tragedy that the conventional model used for God has not very frequently found its centre in this faithful Love. Much of the time our tradition has talked of a divine monarch or ruler who is absolutely in control of the world and is thus to be held responsible for whatever happens in it. Much of the time it has talked also of a divine judge, whose major concern is with the conduct of those who live in the world, determining their guilt and assigning sentences, either of punishment in hell or reward in heaven, sentences against which his creatures have no appeal. Often God has been envisioned as 'the great big man up in the sky', in that he is given the attributes of masculinity which society has developed and is denied, save in some slight degree, the feminine qualities which in our culture have unhappily been regarded as somehow inferior to the masculine ones. God is active, inflexible, adamant, assertive, rather than gentle, tender, receptive, deeply sympathetic. Of course this last picture has been modified somewhat, and of necessity, by the Christian faith in Jesus Christ and in him suffering and crucified. This has meant that some room has been found for talk of God as 'loving'. But for many people this has been more an adjective modifying the substantive noun 'power' than the central clue to God's nature.

When such pictures of God have been dominant, it has been difficult to talk intelligibly of God's being influenced or affected by what happens in the creation. This is because the stress in the pictures is on the divine all-sufficiency, total control, demand for moral rectitude, and active self-assertion, none of which fits in very well with the focus on Love – for love is always a matter of receiving as well as of giving, and it requires that both lover and beloved are involved in a kind of relationship which matters to and has its results for each of them. When we come to consider, in Chapter 7, what I shall call 'God as recipient', much more will be said on this point. For the moment, I wish only to stress the relationship which exists between the divine reality and the finite creatures in the world, whether or not this relationship is always fully grasped and given the correct interpretation.

Granted that there is such an unfailing relationship, one of its chief modes is certainly in God's providing the final dependability in the cosmos. In outlining the meaning of human existence we have spoken of the patent truth that the events in the world, and especially men and women in that world, are dependent and not independent. They are dependent upon their creaturely or human fellows and they are dependent upon the total natural order; without these two, human existence (and any other created existence) would be meaningless. But underneath and through such dependence upon other created entities, there is a dependence upon the divine creativity. One might say that other humans and the world in which we live serve as surrogates for the divine dependability. They are *surrogates*, which is a way of saying that they are agencies by which God works; they are *not substitutes*, although much of the time, in our foolishness and defection, we regard them as such – and in so regarding them bring about a state of affairs which is disproportionate and destructive. To think and act as if such creaturely occasions were divine is to fall victim to idolatry, where the creature is worshipped as if it were the creator. But only God is finally creative and only God is worthy of the worship which is proper towards the supremely unsurpassable and all-encompassing reality 'in which we live and move and have our being'.

This dependability can and does express itself, and receive its due recognition, in specifically 'religious experiences'. Such an understanding is present in Schleiermacher's definition of religion as a sense, feeling, or awareness or human dependence upon God. But there is a wider aspect; and at the moment I am concerned with that wider aspect, with what Whitehead styled the 'secular functions' of deity, recognized as operative in the world but not necessarily the occasion for explicit religious consciousness. There is a special need to emphasize this, because far too often in the thought of religiously-minded people God has become nothing more than an essential, and indeed central, aspect of their faith, without attention to the ways in which God (if he really *is* God) is active in modes that are not thus known or defined. Human existence and human experience are not all that is important in this universe we know or in the creation at large.

In his utter dependability, God is the guarantor of order in the world. God sets the limits, so to say, beyond which the contrasts and varieties of events would become sheer chaos. We talk of *cosmos*, and that signifies exactly such an ordering of things. While there is no absolute determinism, in which everything happens in a mechanical fashion and with no possibility of deviation or modification, there is a patterning. Scientists count upon this for their experiments and explorations; the rest of us take it for granted as providing the context in which our lives are lived. Whatever name we may wish to give this assumption, we all of us do in fact believe in it and we live and act, as we think and speak, in terms of it.

Yet within the basic cosmic continuity which is the result of such an order, there is also the appearance of novelty. Genuinely new things occur. And if the relationship of God and world begins with dependability and goes on to patterning, it also includes the provision of possibilities for the appearance of the new. Such possibilities come from somewhere; they cannot be simply the past which is inherited, for that would mean repetition *without* novelty. But God, from among the countless number of possibilities, as it were selects one which is then a 'given' for an event or particular occasion; this is what Whitehead would call an 'initial aim' which the occasion may then adopt for its own and towards the actualizing of which, in concrete fashion, it may work. Here is a third aspect of the God-world relationship.

Along with that third aspect there goes the way in which each event or occasion in the world is 'lured' (again a Whiteheadian term) towards making its aim actual. From our own experience we are well aware of the many invitation and solicitations, the many pressures and influences, which come to us. They may be rejected or they may be accepted; they may seem attractive and compelling or they may be dismissed as irrelevant and unimportant. None the less, they are there. They constitute part of that God-world relationship about which we are speaking, for they too must have their source in something that is deeply grounded in the way things go in the creation.

Choices may be made in the world which result in distortion or blockage; there are evils, to use the traditional word, which can and do interfere with the realization of a pattern that is good and right. At the human level, there is what we style 'sin' – wilful choice, with

35

its consequences, of that which is self-centred, regardless of other occasions, content to remain stuck in the present without concern for future possibilities – and this is an obstacle which is like an algebraic surd. It does not fit in, it cannot be explained away, it must be faced and dealt with in some fashion. Here again, to meet this obstacle, the God-man and God-world relationship includes what I should wish to speak about as a 'healing operation'. In the natural order this is often seen; damage things as we may, somehow there is yet a restorative activity which works towards a recovering of balance. Doctors talk about the healing work of nature and are prepared to say that their own job is primarily to assist that work to take place. In human relationships themselves, something of the same healing may, and often does, occur. 'Time is the healing river', said W. H. Auden; and there seems to be a way in which the worst of evils, which *as evil* are not to be welcomed nor valued, can be incorporated into some later ordering which may very well be all the deeper and more significant because it has absorbed and used that which in itself was horribly wrong. Probably all of us have had an experience, however slight, of just that healing process in our own lives, when wrongs we have done or intentions for evil to which we have succumbed are strangely and almost miraculously used to give our later life a depth and worth that otherwise it might not have exhibited.

This healing or recuperative process is also part of the continuing relationship between God and the creation. Along with the others to which I have referred, it may now be seen as representing a supreme way in which value, importance, worth, and dignity are provided for, and given to, the things of the world through God's self-identification with them and his reception of them into his own ongoing movement for good. As I have already urged, with a quotation or two from Schubert Ogden, a sense of such value, worth, importance, and dignity is integral to human existence as such. Otherwise we should not go on living. Even when we see someone who feels that his life is meaningless and as a result contemplates and may even commit suicide, there remains that hidden sense of meaning – for to be a suicide *is* to say that at least in this way, if in no other, I may act out meaningfully what I think is worth doing. Most of the time, however, we simply take our creaturely worth as something granted and given; we may not think about it much if at all, yet it is the basis for our existence. This sense of worth or significance is not in itself divine, to be sure; but it is grounded in the divine concern for the creation, and in that concern alone can it find any rational and meaningful explanation.

I have been discussing what have been styled by Whitehead some aspects of 'the secular function' of God in the creation. Now I must say something about the more conscious aspect of relationship which is usually in view when we speak of religion and the practice of religion. Whitehead once suggested that from the religious vision we may conclude that there is a source for, and a giver of, 'refreshment and companionship' to be known and enjoyed by human beings. It seems to me that these two words sum up in a useful fashion what the several religious traditions have offered to their adherents. Their ways of doing this are most varied, ranging from a sense of acting in accordance with the 'rightness in things' (as in much Chinese religion), through a mystical identification of the deepest self or *atman* with the cosmic reality or *brahma* (as in Hinduism), or a 'blowing-out' of individual selfhood by sharing in the bliss of Nirvana (as in most varieties of Buddhism), to the sense of fellowship or communion with God found in our own Jewish-Christian religious tradition. In these quite different ways, something is being said about a refreshment or enablement which is provided for human existence; and something is also being said, even in a fashion which sometimes seems curiously negative (as in Indian religious thought and observance), about a relationship with a more ultimate and all-inclusive reality that establishes a kind of companionship between our own little life and the greater circumambient divine being. Some useful comments about this, especially insofar as Eastern Asiatic culture has things to tell us, can be found in such a study as Trevor Ling's fascinating *History of Religion East and West*, (Macmillan 1969) as well as in the many books of Raymond Pannikar, R. C. Zaehner, Ninian Smart, and S. Radhakrishnan.

Within the Jewish-Christian tradition, this refreshment and companionship is given a supreme and clear statement in the language in which the biblical writers speak of God as the living one who identifies himself with his creatures, works for their healing, enables them to experience newness of life, and enters into fellowship with them. Christians speak of this as taking place 'through Jesus Christ'; and here we have to do with the way in which an event in the historical order, with its setting in the natural world (for all history has a geography, as I have often phrased it in my teaching), has made a genuine difference. The difference has been made in how things have gone in succeeding centuries; and that requires that a difference has been made also for God, since he is affected by what takes place in the world. And *a fortiori* a difference has been made in the possible kind of relationship between that God and the world, such as is opened up by the fact that the event of Jesus Christ has indeed occurred.

What this all comes down to, then, in respect to the main subject of the present book, is that all existence, and particularly for our purposes human existence, stands continually in a genuine relationship with God. God values such existence; God works in and through such existence; God guarantees that such existence has its own dignity in the total scheme of things and that it can make its own contribution to that totality. The cosmic enterprise is like a great adventure, in which deity moves out towards the creatures – not as if it were only an incidental or accidental act of God, but because God by very necessity of the divine nature itself is constantly outgoing, self-identifying, receptive, and responsive. In that sense, then, 'nothing walks with aimless feet' and nothing will be 'cast as rubbish to the void'. What happens *matters*; and those who are the agents of the happening matter also. They are not mere irrelevancies; on the contrary, they count, and they count for exactly what they are and for exactly what they have been and what they have done. And since all 'being' is found only in 'doing' – Whitehead's maxim that 'a thing *is* what it *does*' is crucial here – the creaturely energizing which is at work in the whole creation finds its goal in, and its final significance through its being taken 'up' into himself by the unsurpassable God 'whose nature and whose name is Love'.

In Chapter 7 of this book, on 'God as Recipient', we shall have occasion to spell out more fully the model of God which is implied in what has been said up to the present point. But before we come to that discussion, it will be useful for us to turn our attention to the question of 'resurrection' – first, the resurrection of Jesus Christ, about which so much of the earliest Christian writing found in the New Testament, and so much of the Christian experience of discipleship, turns; and second, to consider the point of the continuing

Christian affirmation that those who have responded to the event of Christ are themselves made 'sharers in Christ's resurrection'.

In any case, it will be evident by now that the relationship between God and the created order is much more like that between the human mind and the human body, as we commonly conceive it, than it is like that between an earthly ruler and his subjects. As I have quoted on other occasions and in other writing, St Thomas Aquinas made the point with his usual precision in an incidental remark – provided perhaps that we change his word 'soul' to the word 'mind'. Aquinas said, 'In his "rule" God stands in relation to the whole universe as the soul stands in relation to the body.' What *that* may imply for 'the risen life' of men and women will be developed in the sequel.

5

Resurrection: Christ 'Risen from the Dead'

The Anglican Book of Common Prayer directs that on Easter Day there shall be sung at the services of the church a special canticle, arranged from portions of St Paul's letters to the Corinthians (I Cor. 5.7 and 12.20) and the Romans (6.9); similar directions are found in the liturgy of other Christian communities. The canticle runs like this:

> Christ our passover is sacrificed for us; therefore let us keep the feast;
> Not with the old leaven, nor with the leaven of malice and wickedness: but with the unleavened bread of sincerity and truth.
> Christ being raised from the dead dieth no more; death hath no more dominion over him.
> For in that he died, he died unto sin once: but in that he liveth, he liveth unto God.
> Likewise reckon ye also yourselves to be dead indeed unto sin: But alive unto God through Jesus Christ our Lord.
> Christ is risen from the dead: and become the first fruits of them that slept.
> For since by man came death: by man came also the resurrection of the dead.
> For as in Adam all die: even so in Christ shall all be made alive.

Thus it is established in a liturgical manner that at the heart of Christian faith is the conviction both that Jesus Christ is 'risen from the dead' and also that 'in Christ' our human existence finds its intended destiny and fulfilment. Christ risen and Christians 'in

Christ': these are the subjects for our discussion in this and the next chapter. The two topics belong together; and together they bring us to the main stress in Christian thinking about the worth or value, the significance and importance, of the lives of human beings, now that the event of Jesus Christ has taken place.

But we cannot leave it there. Neither the resurrection of Jesus Christ nor the 'life in Christ' which it is claimed is available for men and women, can be taken as self-explanatory. Both of them require exploration and explanation, so far as we are able to give this. And the first matter for study is the meaning of resurrection in the case of the Lord in whom Christians find both the decisive disclosure of God and also the empowering from God which they say has brought to them 'newness of life'.

There have been many different ways of interpreting Jesus' resurrection. The simple reader of the New Testament material might assume the obvious interpretation to be the literal coming to life again of the One who died on Calvary. And this might be taken as requiring the literal 'rising' from death of the physical body of Jesus. Unquestionably many have believed just this. But St Paul makes a distinction in I Corinthians 15 between such a 'physical body' and what he styles (in the common English translation of his Greek words) a 'spiritual body'. For him there is a continuity of some sort between the two; yet there is also a difference. He is clear that 'flesh and blood cannot inherit the kingdom of heaven', so for him, the literal physical body of Jesus, with its flesh and blood, cannot be raised from death. But continuous with that physical body, although different from it, there is a 'body' which *can* thus 'inherit the kingdom of heaven'. Evidently it is a 'body' which is appropriate to life in and with God who himself is 'spirit'. And the gospel narratives about the resurrection of Jesus portray a 'body' which was indeed very strange – a 'body' which in one sense is presented as quasi-physical, to be sure, but, which also can appear without movement from place to place, a 'body' which bears the marks of his passion, but which is not exactly the same as the body which hung upon the cross.

Some have said – and doubtless the majority of believers have assumed – that after Jesus' burial there was a rising such that the tomb in which he had been laid was found empty. Others have not been so sure of this supposed fact, but have preferred to stress the

41

appearances of Jesus to his disciples following his death. The way in which these appearances have been understood has also varied from what might seem in effect a materialization of the risen Lord to what have been called 'veridical visions' seen by the disciples, but yet not of the order of obvious manifestations which anybody could have experienced at the time.

Biblical study, of the most exacting sort, can never answer the question of what precisely did happen, nor can it provide the evidence necessary to assure us of the specific and concrete events associated with Jesus' resurrection, whatever they were. What it can do is to work towards a discovery of the earliest strata of material in the gospel narratives, and thus indicate what it is highly likely the earliest disciples believed. For many, if not most, New Testament scholars this has resulted in the belief that the first or most primitive material has to do with the appearances of Jesus; the empty tomb material is secondary, however deeply it may seem to be embedded in the ongoing tradition of which the gospel narratives are the deposit.

It would seem that Paul Tillich is correct in saying that there are several different theological views which believers have held in this respect. The notion of a sheer 'resuscitation', in which the physical body of the Lord was brought to life once again, is one. Another is what might be styled the 'transformation' theory; that is to say, with St Paul (and later with St Thomas Aquinas, for instance), that the physical body was in some wonderful way changed into a 'spiritual body' which could pass through closed doors, be in many places almost at once, and have qualities more characteristic of ghosts than of human existence. Then there is the theory that whatever may have happened to the actual physical body of Jesus, his 'total personality' (as it might be put) is no longer associated with the 'physical integument' (the phrase is Dr H. D. A. Major's) which was its mundane abode, but now continues in such a fashion that it may be known and experienced by others in a genuine communion of persons. And there is also Tillich's own theory: the resurrection really is a statement that the existential Jesus has become, for those who have faith, the essential Christ in whom Godhead and manhood are so united that existential human possibility has become essential manhood or humanity. This is the 'restitution' theory, as Tillich calls it. It is the vindication and validation, by God, as 'the ground of being', of Jesus as the existential manifestation of that 'ground'.

Now these theories are interesting, although as theories they are indemonstrable and can only be accepted on the basis of a particular way of reading the New Testament material, differing according to the assumptions of those who study this material. At least one of them, that suggested by Tillich, depends to a considerable degree upon the Tillichian 'system' in which there is much talk about 'existential' and 'essential' manhood, not to mention the more general philosophical position which he adopts with its talk about 'the ground of being', 'the power of being', and 'the new being in Christ' – the last of these constituting in fact what 'restitution' is all about. For him it is this 'new being', made available through the total fact of the 'biblical Christ', which is established by 'restitution', in that there has now been manifested the basic reality of the divine-human relationship or what might be styled, with some Eastern Orthodox theologians, the truth of 'God-manhood'.

In the writing of Rudolf Bultmann, the great German form-critic whose programme of 'de-mythologization' attracted much attention during the past quarter-century, there is still another way of presenting the meaning of resurrection. For Bultmann, Jesus died on the cross; but he is 'risen in the kerygma' or the preaching of him as the unique 'act of God' the one in whom the past is overcome, the future is opened up, and a new life in faith by grace is made available to those who will respond to the proclamation. This kind of interpretation obviously does not require anything to be said about a 'resurrection body' of any kind. Bultmann is quite prepared to allow that the physical body of Jesus went the way of all human bodies, although at the same time *something* about or of Jesus may have continued – perhaps this would be like the soul, in older Hellenistic idiom, or the 'personality' of Jesus without the 'physical integument'. But questions of this kind appear to the great German scholar to be both irrelevant and meaningless.

Perhaps for Bultmann, certainly for Tillich, there is no absolute requirement that we accept the familiar soul-body dichotomy. On the other hand, in most of the conventional ways of understanding resurrection, such a dichotomy is presumably taken for granted. If it is the 'personality' of Jesus which is raised from death, that must be distinguishable, and in principle separable, from the body which was his in 'the days of his flesh' in Palestine. If the physical body of Jesus was not thus raised, but only a 'spiritual body' which was continuous with, but different from, the physical, then the question can be asked; is this at once united with, part of, or in what other way associated with his soul? The last point assumes considerable importance when we ask just what it is that constitutes a genuinely human existence. I have urged in an earlier chapter that to be human is to be *both* body and soul in a complex relationship in which the soul (or do we mean *mind* here?) is the carrier of the rationality, conation, and capacity for emotional or sensible response. Or are these now to be taken as the essential functioning of the animated, directive, and feeling aspect of experience inembodiment?

These are but a few of the many issues which may be faced if we take the more conventional, and for centuries the popular, view. Obviously with Tillich they are not raised; probably they are not raised for Bultmann. But we should now ask if there is a way in which we can speak intelligibly of 'resurrection' without having such questions to plague us. Of course it *is* possible to say that such questions and many more like them are of the sort that the limited human mind cannot properly discuss; we must accept the reality of the rising of Jesus and simply leave it there. We can say that this is of *faith*; and that it is presumptuous and absurd, perhaps sinful, for finite human minds to try to understand how this rising took place. This may seem to many a suitably reverent attitude. To me it appears to be a sub-human one, for it is based on the notion that human enquiry about the implications of what is proposed in faith, ws well as the honest effort to see what is really being asserted, is to be replaced by little more than pious credulity.

Having thus posed all sorts of questions, legitimate enough if we grant the usual position about resurrection, it is now our task to set forth what may be a more coherent and credible way of thinking about 'Jesus risen from the dead'.

First of all, it should be acknowledged, indeed gladly asserted, that for St Paul at least, and probably for most primitive Christians too, the resurrection of Christ *is central*. For St Paul, it is by his resurrection (however *we* may interpret it) that Jesus is 'declared to be the Son of God'. St Paul does not regard Christian discipleship as the following of the teaching of a human Rabbi, neither does he believe that in such discipleship we have to do with a 'dead' Lord and Master. For him Jesus is the 'living Lord'; he is the Christ of Christian faith quite as much as, probably even more than, the Jesus of history. I am using here two well-known ways of pointing to Jesus Christ. One of these stresses the risen Lord as somehow known within the life of the Christian church, the other puts its main emphasis on the historical figure about whom we read in the Gospels and concerning whom it is taken to be possible to speak with a high degree of historical accuracy.

But to the apostle, such a dichotomy would have made little sense. He apparently has no doubt that there *was* a Jesus of history; at the same time it is not in that figure that he reposes his ultimate trust. On the contrary, he can even go so far as to say on one occasion that 'knowledge of Jesus after the flesh' is *not* the point of Christian faith; that point is the risen Lord who is 'at the right hand of God' and with whom in some way believers may still be in touch. To be a Christian is for St Paul to be 'in Christ', so that while we still remain here in this world we are also able to be 'with' that Christ 'in the heavenly places'.

St Paul and the first Christians did not think in terms of any natural 'immortality of the soul'. Their way of thinking was in terms of the older Jewish belief in 'resurrection of the body' – and hence the only manner in which they could proclaim that Jesus had not been put out of the way through death was to say that he had indeed been 'raised from the dead', that he was in and with God, and that those who belonged to him were granted a share in the risen life which was properly his own. Present relationship with Christ was the point of it all; what had happened to Jesus was, to be sure, important but it was not the heart of the matter. In our next chapter we shall return to this and its significance so far as our own 'resurrection' is accepted in some meaningful sense. For the present, we must emphasize that for St Paul certainly, and doubtless for other primitive Christian believers, relationship with Christ seems to have meant basically relationship with something in or something about God in his inner life and in his unfailing activity in the created order. One way in which this was stated was through St Paul's assertion that Jesus as Christ was in a profound sense one with (even identified with) the 'Wisdom of God' – or in St John's idiom, with the 'Word of God'. Just how we are to understand this language is not entirely clear, but one thing at least is certainly plain. There was *that* in God which had been active in the historical event of Jesus, in the full reality of his human existence; and the *that* was now a continuing and integral reality in God's very existence. What is more, this 'Wisdom' or 'Word' was the divine agency by which God was actively at work in the world, in creation as well as in redemption.

We are not concerned here to consider the eventual result of this Pauline and early Christian interpretation of Jesus – the development of the doctrine of the triunity of God, with distinctions made between the eternal Father, the Word (or Son) as the 'outgoing' of God in creation and redemption, and the Holy Spirit somewhat uncertainly added to round out the three-fold pattern in unity. In another book, *The Divine Triunity* (Pilgrim Press 1977), I have discussed this topic and have sought to make a case for the retention of the triunitarian symbol as precisely *that*, a symbol which has the virtue of safeguarding much that is important in the enduring Christian way of seeing God, the world, and human experience. The point for us in this context, however, is that the New Testament material as a whole enables us to see that the first Christians, or their immediate successors, did not rest content with affirming that Jesus, in himself, was risen; they went on to say that the activity of God in his self-expression, above all in that self-expression in Jesus, was an abiding reality in the creation. What is more that abiding reality was taken to include for ever all that Jesus did and was, all that was effected in and through Jesus – historic teacher, last of the great Jewish prophets, one who 'went about doing good', the crucified and risen Lord, all of these united in the inclusive reality which is named when we use the phrase 'Jesus Christ our Lord'.

The fact of Jesus Christ, therefore, is a total fact, with a unitary quality which makes it include and express (*a*) a human life which was remembered, (*b*) a vital experience of salvation which was enjoyed, and (*c*) the activity of God that was in, through, with, and behind this totality. Or, to put it in another way, the event which is this total fact has not come to an absolute end with the crucifixion. On the contrary, God has received Jesus so that now he 'lives unto God', as the Easter canticle puts it. In God's receiving Jesus into his own life, 'all that appertains to the perfection' of human nature (in a phrase from one of the Thirty-Nine Articles of the Church of

46

England) has also been received and accepted. Thus the notion of resurrection is a way of saying that first in respect to Jesus, and then (as we shall see) in a more general sense, all materiality, all history, and all relationships which have been known and experienced, have been received by God into the divine life. All this, finding focus in the event of Jesus Christ, has been made part of God in his 'consequent aspect' – that is to say, in the concrete sense of God as One who is affected by that which has taken place in the world where he is ceaselessly at work.

Furthermore, this divine reception has been of Jesus as actually and concretely he was, in terms of what actually and concretely he did. Nor is this simply a matter of what could be called 'the dead past'. Far from that, since there could be nothing more vital and living than to be a participant in God's own existence. In what fashion that living quality is preserved and guaranteed is not so important as is the fact itself. But for *God* to remember, to make part of the divine reality (in the serious sense in which we have already spoken and about which more must be said in the sequel), is to bring the past into the immediacy of the present divine awareness, from which nothing can be lost save that which is utterly alien to the divine nature of love – and even then, the divine alchemy can transform that evil into an opportunity and occasion for further good.

The creative movement in the world, in its every detail and its varying degrees of importance, with whatever it has contributed to furthering God's love and his activity in love, is continuously experienced by God, known to him, cherished by him, and used in the furthering of his objective – which is the wider and wider sharing of love, with its related righteousness and truth and in its enduring beauty, in the ongoing of the creative process. Since in Jesus Christ there has been brought to a focal point the significance given by God to the human creation, it is precisely *this* which is 'raised from the dead' and now abides in God for ever. By the italicized *this* in the last sentence I mean to indicate Jesus Christ himself in the integrity of the event which we designate when we name him. But to speak of any event is also to speak of the prior occasions which exerted their causal efficacy upon it, as well as of the future consequences which it has brought about – these two quite as much as the particular circumstances of that event's present moment when and as it took place. This will have its relevance to what must be said in the next chapter, when we come to speak of how one may understand the resurrection of those who are 'in Christ'.

As the present chapter comes to an end, I repeat that what has been attempted here is a 'de-mythologizing' of our inherited conviction about Jesus' own resurrection. There have seemed to be only two final possibilities which may be followed in our approach to that resurrection; it has been assumed that choice must be made between them. *Either* we must accept the stories more or less as they stand, with whatever subtle changes may appear required once we have rejected a literal physical miracle. In that case we are to believe in a transformation of the physical body into a 'spiritual body' or to talk about the persistence through death of either the soul or the 'personality' of Jesus. *Or*, if we do not take this way, we must accept (so it is thought) that there is no such thing as resurrection at all, save in Tillich's attenuated sense of 'restitution' or Bultmann's even more attenuated sense of 'risen in the *kerygma*'. But I have been urging a third way or possibility.

To repeat in substance what has been urged, that third way or possibility is to take very seriously indeed what the stories in the Gospels and in the earliest Christian writing and preaching were concerned to proclaim: that Jesus' death on the cross was *not* the end of the matter, but that, on the contrary, Jesus was somehow seen after that death to 'live unto God'. At the same time, however, we may most satisfactorily grasp the meaning of that life 'unto God' when our model of God is such that God can be believed to receive into himself and to cherish for ever all that Jesus was and did and all that was effected through him. In other words, it is by centring our thought on God and how God has been enriched in his experience of relationship with the human creation, how God now has the possibility through what he has received of being related with that creation at its human level in a new way; it is in *this* fashion that we can give to Jesus 'the highest place that heaven affords'.

This does not mean that God is changed, if by that verb 'changed' it is suggested that the divine nature if altered or becomes something essentially different from what it was before Christ's death and thus moves in and towards the world in a fashion totally at variance with the prior mode of divine concern. This will not do, since God's nature and activity are always and everywhere identically Love-in-act. But new occasions make a difference of another sort. They open up the possibility for God to be related to the creation, and in this instance at the level of human existence, in the light of the new occasion, by the responsiveness of God to that event and by his employment of that event to bestow upon his human children still further 'graces and mercies'. These do not contradict nor deny the 'graces and mercies' which God always bestows upon the world. What they do, however, is to bring them to a vivid and vital focus – to use again the term we have found so helpful – and thus to make them more poignantly available and more decisively effective for God's children.

In principle, such a completely open and enriching relationship has always been possible, and something of it has been realized in the great saints and seers and prophets and sages, even when they would not have used just these words to describe what they knew in the depths of their own experience. But principles need to be given statement in concrete terms, general truths need to have particular illustrations, the divine Lover must be seen in a specially clear instance to *be* such a divine Lover. This, I urge, is what is being affirmed when we speak of the resurrection of Jesus Christ, 'raised from the dead' and 'living unto God'.

6

Resurrection: Our 'Risen Life'

Jesus Christ is 'risen from the dead' and hence he is now and will be for ever participant in and effective for God in his 'consequent aspect' as related to the world. That, I have maintained, is what is being affirmed in the New Testament declaration that he is 'risen'. But the New Testament also makes plain that Christ is not risen *alone*. It is Christ with his 'members', with those who have been incorporated into his 'body' and who are therefore associated with him in this intimate manner, who may be spoken about in such terms.

This at once brings us to a consideration of the significance of the phrase 'in Christ' – a phrase which St Paul uses many (perhaps a hundred times), if we include all the writing associated with his name, excepting of course the Epistle to the Hebrews.

If the fashion in which the basic New Testament proclamation has been interpreted in the preceding chapter has validity, then talk of the resurrection of Christ is a way of affirming that God has received into his own life all that the historical event, designated when we say 'Jesus Christ', has included: his human existence as teacher and prophet, as crucified man upon his cross, in continuing relationship of others with him after that death, and along with this what has happened in consequence of his presence and activity in the world. *All this* has been taken into God; *all this* is immediately known to God; *all this* is treasured in the divine memory; *all this* qualifies whatever we are prepared now to say about God and about the divine relationship with the world and more especially about that relationship as it has to do with human existence.

So, we may ask, what about you and me? What about those of

us who in one way or another have been made 'partakers of the divine nature' through Christ and have in him found newness of life, security and joy in living, and the conviction that we are given worth or value through our intimate association with him? To matters of this sort we must now turn.

Before we do this, however, we need to say something about what in conventional Christian idiom have been styled 'the last things': death, judgment, heaven and hell. Unless we do this, we shall see the entire subject in a disproportionate way. For we shall then be all too likely to dismiss death as a mere incident, to think of judgment without due seriousness, and to regard heaven and hell (our possible human destiny, for good or for ill) as nothing more than 'fairy-tale' talk. Let us then devote a few paragraphs to a serious consideration of those traditional 'last things' and attempt to see what, in their own perhaps odd way, they may have to tell us about ourselves and about human destiny.

First of all, death. In earlier chapters in this book I have probably said enough on this subject. We all will die, I have urged; all of us will die, I have also said. Death is no insignificant incident, to be taken as it were 'in our stride'; rather, it is the finality of our existence, because the book of our life will have been concluded and the final words of that book will have been written. But it is also a sign of the finitude of our human existence; and therefore the recognition and acceptance of it must qualify all that we do in this world. We are expendable; we are not the centre of things; we shall not 'pass this way again', since when the final page is written that is for us the conclusion of the story so far as our wordly existence is concerned. Yet Christian faith would say something more. It would insist that in the very fact of our finitude, symbolized by our death, we still have a value or worth which is *not* destroyed and which in some fashion is persistent in the very structure and dynamic of the universe.

Then we turn to judgment. Day by day we are undergoing judgment or as I should prefer to put it, we are being appraised. We appraise ourselves in the light of our human possibility and we are appraised by others in our relationship with them. We are appraised in terms of what we have or have not contributed to the realization of justice, goodness, and love in the world. Have we, or have we not, made what may be counted as a valuable contribution to that ongoing movement? This is a searching and disturbing question. Even more so is the further question of our having done or not done what was in us to do towards the fulfilment of the divine intention in the creation. When all is said and done, has our existence made any difference in that respect? Can we think, honestly and without special pleading, that we have really *mattered* in the long run? What is there in us and in our achievements which is worthy of preservation in God?

When heaven and hell are brought into the picture, once more we can speak in what might appropriately be called existential idiom. Without projecting all this into some future state 'beyond death', we can ask whether there is here and now some awareness of a movement towards our human fulfilment or, on the contrary, a sense that our human movement is towards futility and meaninglessness? We might say then that heaven, in this present moment, is the realization of our potential humanness; and that hell is the denial of that realization, through our own choices and their inescapable consequences.

Now it will have been apparent that for each of these 'last things' there is both a present and a future reference. 'We die daily': so it is often said, not only with reference to the death of our bodily cells and their replacement by other cells every few years, but also in respect to our possible human growth. In a well-known saying, this time from Tennyson, 'men may rise on stepping-stones of their dead selves'. This is the present reference. But the future one is simply that there comes a time when we do die totally and that this our mundane existence then comes to an end. About that I have spoken often in this book. Likewise with judgment or appraisal. We have seen that we are being appraised in the present; and also that at the end of our days there can be a final appraisement of what, in the long run and after our this-world activities have been brought to their finish, we have really been worth – what we have amounted to, so to say, when everything is taken into consideration.

Then again there is the present reference in talk about heaven and hell; to this we have just referred. But there is also a future one. We might put this simply by saying that either we are, or we are not, taken into the life of God, however we may wish to conceive this 'taking'. In the Bible we are told that God is 'of purer eyes than to behold iniquity'; perhaps this might be re-phrased to tell us that

52

into the divine life evil *as such* cannot be received, while good is *always* received and treasured. In saying this, I have been thinking of evil *as such*, having italicized the 'as such' for it may be (and for Christian faith it must be) characteristic of God as Love-in-act so to exercise his mercy that something that in itself was evil, sinful, or wrong can become by that mercy an occasion for good. This would not deny nor remove the evil, but would put it in to a context where some potentiality for good may be realized. In any event, there is a future reference here which cannot be dismissed merely by talk about 'wishful thinking' or human pretension.

Although not included, strictly speaking, among the 'last things', an intermediate state – commonly called 'purgatory' in the Western Catholic Church – is also part of the more widely accepted picture. In Protestant circles this was rejected, for historically understandable reasons, at the time of the Reformation in the sixteenth century. In our own day, however, there has been some return to the concept among many Protestants, indicated by such practices as the renewed belief that one may pray for those who have departed this mortal life. With Catholic Christians, of course, no rejection ever took place. But what does purgatory mean?

First it has to do with a state supposed to be entered upon at the point of death by those who have in them, so to say, the potentiality of reaching heaven – of attaining fulfilment in and with God and enjoying the vision of God. Before heaven, however, there is a necessary process of cleansing, renovation, and purgation of remnants of the evils committed in mortal existence. Central in the whole concept is the conviction that only those who are 'pure in heart' can 'see God'. Hence a preparation for that vision is required; this purgatory provides.

Just as there is this post-mortem side, there is also an existential aspect which has to do with life in this world. Every man or woman must undergo, even here and now, a process of cleansing, renovation, and purgation. The Christian disciple is not one who has arrived at perfection; he is 'on the way' – and this requires what traditionally is called 'mortification' or the killing of whatever is unworthy and the 'sanctification' or development of whatever is good. Thus we might say that 'mortification' and 'sanctification' – becoming holy, through response to God's action – is the earthly counterpart of the purgatorial process. The conception, then, has its double aspect, as do death, judgment before and following death, and heaven and hell. Interestingly enough, what is suggested here is the same point upon which we have already insisted: that life for human beings is a process of 'becoming' and is not to be understood as an entirely completed and finished affair.

All this must be borne in mind when we come to consider human destiny and what might be beyond our death. We should remember that to be human is to be compounded of body and a rational capacity, along with the equally important capacity to act by willing and the reality of our deep human sensitivity or aesthetic awareness. To speak of personal identity needs also to be properly understood from our position. It is not a matter of a substantial ego to which experiences 'happen', so that we might detach the former from the latter after the fashion suggested in the common notion of immortality of the soul when that soul has been 'separated' from the body. But then such a soul would not really be the identical self that existed before such separation; and it was part of the insight of Thomas Aquinas to see that to talk meaningfully of a personal life after death must involve the soul (should it exist at all) or the self in and with the bodily vehicle or organ which, on that theory, it had possessed and must once again possess in some post-mortem state. Of course for Thomas and for traditional thought more generally, we have seen that there were problems at this point. What could be said about a post-mortem soul's existence until the time when it was re-united with a transformed body? And what was happening to the body before that transformation? Questions like this may well be taken as arguing against the general presuppositions with which Aquinas was working.

Furthermore, if we recall that to be human is to be social, so that our relationship with others is integral to and largely constitutive of our own identity, then our thought about survival of death must be very different from the highly individualistic view so popular in the past. Something much more like the 'communion of saints' must be accepted. If here and now I am myself a personal identity only through my living with, by, towards, and from other personal identities – and indeed by my contacts with the entire natural order from which I am an emergent but of which I still remain as a part – then those others and that order must have their place in the picture. Indeed the very phrase 'communion of saints' can also be translated, when we consider the Latin *communio sanctorum* and the Greek *koinonia hagion*, as signifying 'participation in holy things'. While in its original use this was probably a reference to sacramental participation in the consecrated bread and wine of the eucharist, there is a possible further extension of its meaning so that it will include a relationship with the whole natural order, seen as a sphere of the divine activity and hence as a way of contact with the God who is operative within it. Here the insight of some of the Eastern Orthodox divines may be of help to us, not to mention the fashion in which (to give one example) we find Father Zossima in *The Brothers Karamazov* speaking of the holiness of the very dirt under his feet and of everything else that surrounds him in the non-human creation.

These considerations will once again come to the fore when in the latter part of this chapter I make some positive suggestions as to human destiny after death. For the moment, however, let us turn to the New Testament stress on the relationship of the believer with Jesus Christ himself. In the Pauline literature much stress is laid on membership in the 'body of Christ'. This means the church, to be sure; but it would be absurd to think that by saying 'the church' we are pointing to the institutional establishment which goes by that name. Such an organized body is indeed part of the picture, but the 'mystical body of Christ' (in the well-known liturgical phrase) is not *identical* with it. The church in the Pauline sense may be defined as Christ in and with his members. If the Epistle to the Ephesians is Pauline in outlook, this suggests also that for him and for his interpreters Christ *without* or *apart from* his members is not really Christ at all. So likewise with the Johannine image of the Vine and its branches. In this image the Vine is Christ himself; the branches are those who, so to put it, 'belong to the Vine'. They are Christ's people. A vine with *no* branches would be a very strange vine; but so also would branches which belonged to no vine be very odd. The two go together. And it would be correct to say that the Christian reality for the Johannine writer is vine-and-branches as one total entity, just as for the Pauline writer of Ephesians and for St Paul himself that reality is head-and-members, Christ with his people.

It is not easy to re-state the point of these images in prosaic idiom. Indeed, it is probably quite impossible to do so at all, since their meaning is conveyed through imaginative or poetical insight. But at least we can make some suggestions as to what these images have to tell us in our concrete experience.

First of all, I believe that we can say that we have to do here with the response which is being made to 'the love of God which was in Christ Jesus'. That response brings about a uniting of the human with the divine Love. The divine Love was enacted in and expressed through the event of Christ; and that event was so much tied in with the activity of God that it could not be defeated, even by death with all its horror and loss. Now to be caught up into union with such Love, with God as Love-in-act, is 'eternal life', in the phrase used in St John's Gospel. Hence there is a sort of 'eternality' which is integral to such life in union. Conversely, one who has begun to live 'in love' has also begun to live 'in Love' – that is, to live in God, and in God as he has disclosed himself in the event of Jesus Christ. There is no other God than *that*; and God, so understood, is not confined to the Christ-event but is universally at work and hence universally present. The significance of the event of Christ, understood in this context, is that it defines in a vivid and classical instance what God is always and everywhere 'up to' in his creation.

In the second place, to be 'in Christ' is to be so much at one with the reality enacted and expressed in his human existence that this reality 'comes alive' in those who are his members. It is their 'principle of life', something much more profound than can be indicated by talk about their goodness of life and their concern for righteousness, truth, and the other virtues. To be a 'saint', in New Testament thinking, is not merely to be a moral person, although most of us have been led by inadequate teaching to assume that this is what is meant. But on the contrary, for the New Testament a 'saint' is a man or woman or child who so fully belongs to God in Christ through a continuous response to his impact upon one, that the very Love which is God is the central and all-controlling principle of existence. In such a man or woman or child, what William Law once styled 'the process of Christ' is at work with signal efficacy. Most of us, let us honestly confess, are pretty poor specimens here; there is so much of the 'old Adam' in us that this 'new Adam' has to struggle for expression. But the deepest truth about us is that there *is* this principle of Love-in-act working in us. The horror of our existence is that we are not always or even usually ready to let

Love's work be done without our opposition and our refusal to cooperate and thus to increase our willing response.

Yet this sanctification (as theology phrases it) is never in isolation; it takes place in community, so that to belong to that Love is to be together with our brothers and sisters who each in his or her own way is also responding, however partially and imperfectly that may be. It is here that the 'communion of saints' comes alive in our thinking, not just as something which may be true after our death but as something which is the case in the here and now of our Christian discipleship. And it is here, too, that we may sense our wider belonging with the whole created order, natural as well as historical or human. Thus to share in the Love that is God is to be one with the 'rightness of things', to be in accord with the 'grain of the universe', with a responsibility to reverence the creation and a readiness to care for it in its creaturely integrity.

Yet we live in the midst of a 'perpetual perishing', and we ourselves will have an ending. What then may happen to us as well as to the world itself? Here Christian faith, interpreted with the help of the process conceptuality, can come to our aid. What does it have to tell us?

Some words of Whitehead's are relevant. I quote from *Process and Reality*: 'The image – and it is but an image – the image under which [God's creative working] is best conceived, is that of a tender care that nothing be lost. The consequent nature of God is his judgment on the world. He saves the world as it passes into the immediacy of his own life. It is the judgment of a tenderness which loses nothing that can be saved. It is also the judgment of a wisdom which uses what in the temporal world is mere wreckage' (Cambridge University Press 1928, p. 525).

In Whitehead's words just quoted we have a statement of the way in which according to the understanding of things from a process perspective, the value and worth of the achievements in the creation are both established and preserved. To that kind of understanding the specifically Christian faith makes an addition which provides a much more adequate assurance about such establishment and preservation. For Christian faith has to do with the nature of God as disclosed in the event of Christ. The divine nature, like the divine activity, must then be grasped as nothing other than the 'pure unbounded Love' which in Jesus was vividly manifested, as

57

he has been responded to and as through him a vivid and decisive enabling of human life has been made possible. This brings with it the conviction that such a God – the only God there is – can be trusted to do what is necessary if that phrase about his losing 'nothing that can be saved' is to be meaningful. In the simplest sort of language God is certain to do everything that can be done to give abiding significance to human, as to all other, existence. God's 'tender care' is ceaselessly concerned to give worth and value to the creation; and even more profoundly, God does this by taking the world's accomplishments, and also those who have done the accomplishing, into 'the immediacy of his own life'.

God remembers; and what is in the divine memory is no incidental or accidental matter, but the very reality of the creation kept in him for ever and hence 'come alive', as we might put it, in God's ongoing reality. David Edwards, Dean of Norwich Cathedral in England, has put this point in moving words: 'Certainly one great advantage of thinking about God's memory of us is that it helps us to see that our eternal life is more than this life going on for ever; it is a share in God's life and God's glory, when nothing is between God and us' (*Asking Them Questions*, Oxford University Press 1973, p. 56). Edwards then goes on to ask, 'Does that involve what is commonly called "personal survival"?' To this he replies, '. . . not if that phrase means that no big difference is made by death . . . [but] God will continue to love *you*, the *you* he knows, and *you* will have your own place in the glory of God!'

In this sense, then, Jesus Christ himself is remembered by God; and those who are 'in Christ', as members of his Body or as branches of the Vine which he is, are also remembered. For my part, I am concerned that it is this which is the absolutely central Christian affirmation, not least because the stress is laid on God and on God's action, rather than on ourselves and our 'conscious' awareness of such 'being remembered'. Certainly it is legitimate to entertain the pious hope that in our being thus remembered there may be some kind of 'conscious' awareness. But it is not legitimate, and to my mind it is quite mistaken, to talk as if without such an awareness on our part there is only a 'second best'. To be incorporated into the life of Christ and hence to be taken into the divine remembrance of Christ: here is the heart of genuinely Christian hope, whatever

58

else we may think proper to desire and (in a secondary sense) hope for.

But this must raise the question about what 'happens' to those who have not known Jesus Christ, unlike those of us who are plainly the conscious members of his body. The answer ought to be plain enough. The God who in the event of Christ is disclosed and active is the God who can be trusted to do what is for the best of *all* his children, whether or not they have the explicit knowledge of him which we who are Christians believe has been granted to us. Doubtless there will be included in the divine memory, and hence in the divine life, countless millions who have never had the privilege which we know to have been our own. It is not for us to 'close the gate of heaven' to others; and one of the worst features of conventional Christian teaching has been the all too frequent assumption that until and unless such persons have been brought, usually by our own efforts, it is thought, to share in such explicit knowledge they are 'lost'. The missionary concern of the Christian fellowship, when that fellowship is true to its deepest insight, makes no such claim. Rather, that concern is to share with others, so far as this is possible for us, the joy of Christian discipleship and thus *to give a name* to whatever enablement, ennoblement, and enrichment of life those others may have experienced.

Finally, we should urge that the place where and the time when the Christ who is for ever integral to God's ongoing life is most plainly made integral also to our own human existence, is the Lord's Supper, the eucharistic action, the Holy Communion. As we 'make the memorial' and enter upon the remembrance of the death of Christ, his resurrection, and his 'ascension' into the life of God, the reality of that total Christ, with all its redemptive power, 'comes alive' for us. It is not without significance that in the New Testament narratives of the resurrection of Christ, it is said (as in the story of the walk to Emmaus in St Luke's Gospel) that 'he was known to them in the breaking of the bread'. *There* in that eucharistic action the Lord 'risen from the dead' becomes the living reality which gives us the assurance of *our* being 'in Christ' and therefore through him participant in God's never-failing remembrance. If 'by faith with thanksgiving' we know ourselves to be indeed 'very members, incorporate in his mystical body', we need have no fear that God will forget us. In the most complete way possible, we may dare to say, we have the assurance of life in and with God, in the mode which preserves both the integrity of the divine nature as Love and also the value and worth of our finite human existence.

7

God as Recipient

In the way of seeing things found in process thought, God is taken to be the chief causative agency in the creation. But he is not the only cause, since every 'actual entity', in Whitehead's idiom – or, as we might say, every occurrence, occasion, or energy-event – has the capacity to exercise a certain creativity. That is only another way of affirming that each of these is able to make significant decisions, in the sense of adopting *this* possibility and rejecting *that* one. And a decision once made brings consequences which must be reckoned with. But God exercises a special kind of causative activity, to be sure, in that he is the source of all novelty through his offering lures or invitations for the creature's decisions, and also the guarantor of the order or patterning which prevents the world from descending from significant and enriching contrast into meaningless and damaging conflict beyond hope of recovery.

But God is also the *chief receptive agency* in the creation. Whatever is done, and wherever or by what or whom it is done, makes a difference to God. For process thought, this is taken to mean that God is not only that One who effects things; he is also the One who is affected by things. He remains always God, to be sure. Nothing can surpass him, nothing can make him less than utterly adorable, nothing can diminish his divine nature with its faithfulness and its utterly loving concern in creative action. Yet the accomplishments of the created order are received by him into his own life, and to them he responds by making use of them for the furthering of his divine intention.

One way of affirming this is by speaking, as we have done, of the divine memory. Whitehead's associate and interpreter Charles

Hartshorne has used this concept; and their followers in the process way of thinking have found it a useful and illuminating idea to employ in understanding how God is affected by the world. Further, we have argued that the notion of divine memory enables us to say something helpful in our attempt to see how that which takes place in the world, and not least in human existence as we know it, can have an abiding value in God.

God's receiving the world's achievements into his own everlasting life; God's remembering for ever that which is thus received; God's using for further good the achievements which have taken place in the created order – here are points which need to be emphasized when we begin to think of the worth or value of human existence. I quite realize the difficulty which some have found in the stress on the divine memory. Generalizing from our own experience, they say that memory is not a very secure basis for establishing that worth. Furthermore, they can easily parody the whole position so that (as one critic, a friend of mine who is not unsympathetic to the wider process conceptuality, has phrased it) talk about divine memory may be taken as nothing more than indicating God's continually re-playing some old film or continually listening to some old soundtrack. But Old Testament writers had a very different and a much more profound understanding of memory in God, as indeed also of memory among us humans.

For an ancient Jew memory seems to have been given what may well be styled a certain causal efficacy. 'To remember' was to make some event in the past 'come alive' in the present. Obviously the Jew did not think that in some outlandish way the past was actually re-played nor did he believe that what had happened in that past was, by its 'being remembered', made in actual concrete fact a contemporary occurrence. What he did believe, we may say, is that the past could be made effectual, significant, and genuinely a causative agency in the present situation. But if that were the case with human memory, even more was this true in the *divine* memory. A good instance is the prayer of Nehemiah, who asks that his God 'will remember him for good'. That is to say, Nehemiah is portrayed as believing that for *God* to have vividly before him, in its importance, something done in this world – in Nehemiah's case his dedication to the rebuilding and welfare of the city of Jerusalem; for God to have that as part of the divine memory was to establish the accomplishment for ever. It had become part of the divine life, so to say; it now and to the end of time would qualify that life. Thus God was indeed 'the God of Abraham, Isaac, and Jacob'. These patriarchs had lived, and fulfilled their vocation, had done that which God purposed for them to do; now they were unforgettable, not only in the trite and obvious sense that they were great men with great achievements to their credit, but in the much more serious sense that they had altered for ever 'how things were to go' between God and the world and between the world and God.

It is obvious, then, that my earlier phrase about the past 'coming alive in the present' was not lightly chosen. Consider present-day Jewish observance. When a contemporary member of the people of Israel observes the Seder at Passover time, he or she is explicity 'remembering' what the religious tradition says took place in the exodus from Egypt, in the crossing of the 'sea of reeds' (as the Hebrew puts it, *not* 'the Red Sea') and in the hurriedly eaten meal of the Jews as they made their escape from the persecution of the Egyptian ruler. It is not at all – for this devout modern Jew – simply a reminiscence which it is helpful to bring to mind and about which there can be talk at that sacred meal. As the family group shares in the food, as the answer is given to the question put by a child there present as to just what this meal is intended to commemorate, *something happens*. The deliverance of those who later took themselves to be 'the chosen people' is re-enacted and made vividly contemporary. Those present at the Seder are made participant in the deliverance; it is *they*, quite as much as their ancestors in the remote past, who know and experience God's arm as 'mighty to save'.

Furthermore, by asking, as is done always at that meal, that *God* remember what was done in that past event, the Jews are expressing the conviction that in the never-failing memory of their God what was done at the first Passover is integrally part of what we might well style, in our own modern idiom, the divine experience. *God is* the God who has done these things; *God is* the God who has accepted his people in their covenant with him made after their deliverance; *God is* the God who can never be understood as existing save seen as related to, and worshipped as the One who is *their* God. What was done in the remote past, therefore, is alive in God; and it also 'comes alive' for God's people as they, in their succeeding generations, bring it to remembrance. Things make a difference *for* God; they make a difference *in* God too. This is not to say, of course, that the divine becomes more divine: for the Jew God is always unsurpassably God. Yet God is the One who values and uses, because God incorporates into the divine life which is everlasting the good that takes place in the historical sequence; and God over-rules or uses *for good* that which comes from the 'vain imagination of foolish men' in their sin and defection – and, we may add, from anything else that is evil or wrong thanks to the free decisions made by the creatures in their divinely granted capacity to choose among relevant possibilities.

I find it impossible to understand how this view can be dismissed by some people as superficial or trivial. I take it to be something which, far from being of little value, is in truth of quite enormous value in our attempt to come to some understanding of God's way of securing permanent validity for that which otherwise would be nothing other than an instance of the 'perpetual perishing' which patently marks the world as we know it. In particular, it seems to me that this way of looking at things helps to make sense of the talk about resurrection, both of Christ and of those who are 'in Christ'. We might say that we have here an eminent instance of the 'de-mythologizing' of an ancient religious conviction; but along with that we have a re-statement of its point in an idiom which preserves its essential meaning but does not fall victim to the charge of outlandish mythological portrayal.

Human existence comes to an end; the last word on the last page of the book of our life is written. But that is not the end of the story in an *ultimate* sense. It is indeed the end, so far as your and my subjective selfhood is concerned, with conscious awareness, with the capacity consciously to act and to choose, and with everything else that is found in our mundane world of space and time. Yet we have been able to find a way of asserting the abiding worth of our mortal span of years, such that our having existed at all can be said to have had dignity and value. In a profound sense there can be *no end at all*, since the God who has accepted, received, and responded to this is the One of whose days there is neither beginning nor ending. For God thus to remember – to treasure and keep in his own everlasting life, as a process conceptuality will claim is done – is for the data which are remembered to abide for ever. Or, in the language of resurrection, they have been 'raised up into' God's life, just as through the initiating lures and the circumambient invitations upon which these creaturely events acted there was a 'coming down' or (if you will) an 'incarnating' activity of God.

To give such strong emphasis to the conception God as recipient requires, as we have seen, a radical change in the model which we use for understanding who God is. At this point I should like to quote from a recent book by John B. Cobb, Jr. and David Griffin, *Process Theology: An Introductory Exposition* (Westminster Press 1976). In their introductory chapter or foreword, Cobb and Griffin speak of the models for God which to their mind must be rejected, to be replaced by a model which is more appropriate both for Christian faith and for a process conceptuality. There are five popular models which they reject. Here they are:

1. *God as Cosmic Moralist*. At its worst, this notion takes the form of the image of God as divine lawgiver and judge, who has proclaimed an arbitrary set of moral rules, who keeps records of offences, and who will punish offenders. In its more enlightened versions, the suggestion is retained that God's most fundamental concern is the development of moral attitudes. This makes primary for God what is secondary for humane people, and limits the scope of intrinsic importance to human beings as the only beings capable of moral attitudes. Process theology denies the existence of this God.

2. *God as the Unchanging and Passionless Absolute*. The notion of 'impassibility' stressed that deity must be completely unaffected by any other reality and must lack all passion or emotional response. The notion that deity is the 'Absolute' has meant that God is not really related to the world . . . the God-world relationship is purely external to God . . . the world contributes nothing to God, and . . . God's influence upon the world is in no way conditioned by divine responsiveness to unforseen self-determining activities of us worldly beings. Process theology denies the existence of this God.

3. *God as Controlling Power*. This notion suggests that God determines every detail of the world. . . Process theology denies the existence of this God.

4. *God as Sanctioner of the Status Quo*. This . . . characterizes a

strong tendency in all religions. It is supported by the three previous notions. . . To be obedient to God is to preserve the *status quo*. Process theology denies the existence of this God.

5. *God as Male*. God is totally active, controlling, and independent, and wholly lacking in receptiveness and responsiveness . . . God seems to be the archetype of the dominant, inflexible, unemotional, completely independent (read 'strong') male. Process theology denies the existence of this God (pp. 9–11).

To this listing, so well made by Cobb and Griffin, I should wish to add two other models which seem to me to be found in much of the conventional talk of deity. One of these is God as the remote creator, who once upon a time in the far distant past 'created the world' but since then has left it to go more or less on its own way, provided, of course, that it follows the laws which (as a hymn puts it) 'never shall be broken'. We might call this the 'Newtonian God', whose only interference in the world, if those are the right words, occurs when God is required to set right a defect which develops in the functioning of the creation. The other model is God as the kind of sentimental love which makes no demands, has no requirements, bends to every pressure, and can become the 'smothering love' which precisely because of its 'softness' is subtly able to control and dominate others and to make any genuine assertive activity on the part of the creatures well-nigh impossible. This view of God has its parallel in the horrible spectacle of a mother or a father who has no firmness nor real integrity and who can ruin children by providing neither true dependability nor persisting purpose. Paradoxically, such a parent effectively denies to the child any genuine independence – as many of us have so often seen in our own observation or experience.

Cobb and Griffin propose a quite different model for God, a model which is in entire agreement with what has been urged in this book and about which I have written more fully in my *God: Models Old and New* (to appear in 1981 from Pilgrim Press, New York). They call this model 'God as Creative-Responsive Love'. I have called it the model of God as 'the Cosmic Lover'; but I welcome these writers' spelling it out in their speaking of that Lover as both 'creative' and 'responsive'. My only addition would be the insistence that God is also 'receptive'. Indeed Cobb and Griffin not only recognize this but insist upon it, although they do so in somewhat different terms. Their proposal is in accordance with all other representatives of process thought when employed by Christian theology.

The several false ways of thinking about God, to which we have just given attention, are in one sense only a projection from the human mind at its worst. As Voltaire said, the ideas of God which are entertained by people are images of what such people think to be highest or most worthy in their own experience: 'God created man in his own image; and men have returned the compliment,' said the French satirist. But the first part of the Voltairean saying, drawn of course from the Bible, also needs attention. What does it mean to speak of humans as 'created in the image of God'? I believe that the basic meaning is that human existence reflects, or is believed to reflect, the essential nature of God. And if we are prepared to affirm that God's essential nature is sheer love, then we can go on to say that human nature is potentially a reflection of that love, although inevitably in a finite and limited, and equally in a defective, fashion.

On the other hand, there is a sort of reflexive movement, so that when such love is seen as the potential reality of human existence, this then becomes also the quality which in human experience is more likely to be esteemed and expressed in action. To think of God as Love-in-act is to say that those who are 'in the divine image' are also intended by that God to be themselves lovers-in-action. But we can also see how the same procedure brings about less happy consequences with respect to the 'models' of God which, as I have urged, process theology must reject and which, as I have also said, the deepest insight of the Jewish-Christian tradition would also reject.

If God is conceived as cosmic dictator, this notion is a reflection of the human desire to control and manage. At the same time, the acceptance of such a picture augments even more strongly this human desire. So also if God is taken to be passionless and uninfluenced, we have a reflection of the human desire to exist without any influence from others and to abstain from the sympathetic participation in other lives which might bring pain and sorrow. Yet once God is conceived in that way, this human desire is strengthened, and men and women can think that such unfeeling

Stoicism and such an unaffected attitude are right and proper for them. If God is taken to be the cosmic moralist, this is a projection from the human wish to judge and through such judgment to reward or punish in terms of the degree to which other persons 'live up to' our own ideas of what is correct. Once this notion of God is entertained, that judgmental stance then receives renewed strength in the lives of men and women.

Again, when God is pictured as the guarantor of the validity of things as they are (in Cobb's and Griffin's words, the *status quo*), we can readily see how this is tied in with the kind of reactionary conservatism which, as Whitehead once remarked, is fighting 'against the cosmic process'. It is indeed a kind of defence used by such people to protect their own interests and refuse all change. Yet when God is interpreted in this fashion, the consequence is that such a negative attitude towards novelty and change is given augmented power and those who think in this way consider their own established interests divinely approved and heavenly sanction given to their own rejection of developments which would call these interests in question. Once more, the idea that God is to be modelled exclusively after so-called masculine characteristics is readily seen to be the way in which males who are fearful of, or threatened by, more feminine qualities protect themselves. God then becomes the supreme instance of machismo. When this happens, the aggressively masculine stance and the dislike of women's having their part and place in the affairs of the world – and in religious communities, the refusal to give women a full share in the communities' life and in their ordained ministry – are taken to be supported by the cosmic order and hence given a divine force in human affairs.

It is likewise in respect to the two concepts which I have added to those mentioned by Cobb and Griffin – the remote creator in time past and the 'smothering' or sentimental kind of so-called (but miscalled) love. The God who created in the past and then left things to go on on their own, save for occasional remedial acts, well represents the way in which some men and women prefer to stand aside from others, yet insist on making occasional (and often disastrous) intrusions into the life of those others. That picture, once accepted, gives greater vigour to the human attitude in question. On the other hand, the notion of God as sentimental niceness – what I have called 'smothering love' – springs from the wish of

68

many people to be so completely tolerant that they are unwilling or unable to take a stand on anything. If God is taken to be like that, it then follows that human love itself is interpreted as being 'Pollyanna-ish' sentimentality, prepared to accept whatever happens, tolerant of anything, however vicious, and utterly lacking in vertebrate strength. And as I urged above in first speaking of this particular picture, the paradoxical consequence is that it is in precisely this kind of spineless attitude that we find a vicious control and possession of others, particularly of those nearest and dearest to the sentimentalist.

I have engaged in this lengthy discussion of 'models of God' for one reason. What sort of God is it, we must enquire, about whom we are talking when we speak of a relationship which will give value and worth to human existence? The concepts which have been rejected cannot do this, for they seem all to place that existence in a position where it is acted upon but can never react to deity. There is no dignity, no importance, no genuine contribution made by the created being; hence relationship with God must be purely one-sided, entirely external. God could not then receive *into himself*, and make part of the divine life, the creatures which are so much outside that life that they are indeed not worthy and not valued.

It is different when we think of God as the cosmic Lover who is receptive and responsive. It is different also when we take for one of our analogies the way in which the mind works in and upon the body and the body acts with and for the mind. When such a picture of God is central to our thinking, we are able readily to appreciate how the divine can receive and give a place to the human. We can also readily appreciate how the divine can work with the human and how the human can work with the divine, in what is in fact a common life or fellowship. Men and women are then seen to be 'co-creators' with God, as Whitehead put it; and as such they are both the creatures of God's love and the sharers in God's ongoing purpose of good in the creative advance.

Rupert Brooke, the English poet of the early years of this century, spoke of his belief in this worth, value, and dignity. He was writing, in the now largely forgotten sonnet 'The Soldier', about his own feeling concerning death in 'a foreign land'. And he said that he would hope that he might be 'a pulse in the eternal Mind'. Now to some this will appear a very unsatisfactory sort of statement. It will appear minimal, at the best. And so it would be, if the 'eternal Mind' were simply some vast and characterless cosmic 'thought'. But if this 'eternal Mind' is the rich, pulsating, loving, living, faithful, yearning, compassionate reality which our talk of the creative-receptive-responsive cosmic Lover has indicated, the story is quite different. To be so much participant in *that* Mind that one is, as it were, 'a pulse' in *its* vibrant life would be a destiny wonderfully appealing.

When to this we add what has been said in the preceding chapter about the 'risen life' in God, made specifically available to men and women through their participation in Jesus Christ 'risen from the dead', we have a 'de-mythologized' portrayal of what 'happens after death' which speaks deeply to authentically Christian faith. God does that which is best; he can be trusted to do just this. And what could be better than the assurance of acceptance by God, in the fullness of what we have been and done, and granted a place in God's life where our human accomplishments are safely preserved for ever?

8

Conclusion and Summary

Unless the discussion in the preceeding pages has entirely failed to make its point, it will be plain that what is being proposed in this book is (as I have said) a 'de-mythologizing' of the inherited notions of 'life after death', with their (to many of us) impossible assertions; and also the 're-mythologizing' – or better, the re-conceiving – of their implicit intention so that we may have a valid way of affirming the value and worth of human existence, its significance and importance for God, and its preservation in God as a reality which has affected the divine life and in God has acquired an enduring quality which nothing can take away.

That is a long sentence, but it states the main purpose of our discussion. In order to arrive at such a re-conception it has been necessary to question the usual ideas about 'subjective immortality' and the pictures in which they have usually been communicated. It has been necessary to consider the nature of God and the relationship between God and the creation, above all the human level of that creation. It has been necessary to see what may be made of the 'resurrection' about which the New Testament speaks, both in respect to Jesus Christ as the decisive event in the story of that divine-human relationship and also in respect to the human side of the matter, where you and I may fit in and have our part and place.

The conclusion of our treatment has been a stress upon God as recipient, who takes into himself, and by thus receiving gives abiding value to, what happens in the created order. For after all, in any faith which is genuinely theocentric or focused upon God, it is essential to make sure that it is *God*, not human desires or wishes or aspirations as they now stand, who is to be 'given the glory';

71

and it is in God, and in God alone, that we may speak meaningfully of the significance of our own existence.

As I have said again and again, one of the religious difficulties with much in the conventional talk of life 'after death' has been a forgetting of this centring upon God. It has almost been as if we humans, with our limitations and in our finitude, not to mention our obvious and tragic defection from right alignment with the divine intention for the world and for us, were to insist that until and unless *we* are given what we regard as due recognition and the security of our own survival in an individualistic sense, we shall refuse to take our place and play our part in the creative advance of the universe. This 'dog-in-the-manger' attitude has nothing to commend it. Who are we to insist that we must receive our reward and be seen to receive it, or else we shall categorically decline to offer service to the divine purpose? To think, act, and speak in that fashion is to presume that we are indeed lords of the whole creation and that what may, or may not, happen to us is what determines once and for all whether the whole enterprise is worth-while.

This is not to say that there may not be motives for our desire for such individualistic survival that cannot be dismissed out of hand as entirely self-centred. To care enough for others to feel that we cannot envisage *their* value as lost is only natural. But there may be another way in which that value is preserved; and in this book we have sought to present the possibility which fits in with general biblical thinking and which is also sufficiently in accordance with the conceptuality we have accepted. Yet it always remains hard to learn the lesson that it is God that matters most and that not even our deepest concern for those whom we have loved unselfishly and generously can be given central place.

Let me say then that to be received into, made an integral part of, and gladly employed by God for his own wonderful enrichment and for the enhancement of his working in the creation, is a destiny such that we can feel nothing other than gratitude and delight in its prospect. This certainly is for the best; nothing could be more splendid, nothing more rewarding, than the confident assurance that we matter to God and that he is both able and willing to use what we have done, and hence what we are, for the further expression of the love which is the divine nature and purpose.

If for a moment I may speak for myself, I must confess that finally to be brought to see things in this way has been a great release from confusion and worry. When one has experienced the death of many of those for whom one has most cared, and when one has been troubled by the thought that they may indeed have gone into the darkness without remembrance, it comes as a great consolation to recognize that in God nothing can be lost. And when the more conventional talk, so familar and often (alas) so superficial in its attempt at securing some permanent value for those loved persons, has been subjected to the kind of critical analysis which is proper to any inherited belief however long it has been cherished, and in consequence has been dismissed as both unconvincing and incredible, then the certain conviction that *in God* – and I repeat this once more – the value of human existence is guaranteed and the worth of all those for whom one has cared is assured, becomes an abiding and unshakeable occasion for joy.

It was to state just that conviction, I believe, that the older pictures were devised. But it is not necessary for us, once those pictures have been rejected as impossible, to give up the basic assurance. I have remarked earlier that all too often it seems that we are presented with two supposedly exclusive alternatives. *Either* we accept, as they stand or with some subtle and dubiously sophisticated modification, the older ways of picturing it, *or* we give up altogether any notion of a value integral to human existence. So it is said or implied. My point in this book has been to indicate that there is another possibility; and that this possibility depends upon a doctrine of God – a model for the divine, worshipful, and unsurpassable reality – which differs from the usual one but which does in fact provide exactly the guarantee for which we yearn. How this is to be presented to our contemporaries is a matter for those who are given the pastoral care of men and women and children. On the one hand, they dare not talk as if our human wish for enduring value were nonsense; on the other, they need to find ways in which the sort of understanding which has been presented here will come home to those who mourn, quite as much as to those who need reassurance about their own significance in the total scheme of things. I conclude, therefore, with a summary statement of the position which seems to me to make sense.

Let me first say that the kind of 'de-mythologizing', followed by re-conception, which I have been urging in this book does not imply

73

that for every detail in the conventional picture we are obliged to find some equivalent in terms of our different perspective. What is at stake is the reality to which the whole picture points. Doubtless many of the details in that picture are gone beyond recovery in any sense whatever. At the same time, I am convinced that nothing of abiding value will be lost; and for myself I can say that I find, even in such concepts as purgatory – which to some might appear incredible in the new concept – something that is not without significance. To put this more plainly, the notion of growth or development, of movement or process, which purgatory affirms of life *after* death, is certainly valid for our experience in the present world. What is more, it is by no means impossible, in the new setting, to see that in God himself there may be an action in which the values achieved in this world, along with the persons who achieve them, are more and more fully received and used, as the wisdom which belongs to eternal Love takes and finds signficance in them. God is not static; he is dynamic and living. Hence we have every right to think that in that dynamic life which is unsurpassable and hence divine there is, not a becoming *more* divine, which would be absurd, but an increasing capacity for finding occasions through which God may employ, in one way or another, that which is always remembered; and also, in this very action as it continues on in God's relationship with creation, a growing acceptance of those who have contributed to the cosmic enterprise of love at work in creation.

And so to our summary. The affirmation which Christian faith must make has to do with relationship with God, here and hereafter. To have one's final destiny in God's reception and in God's employment of all that one has done, and hence all that one is, is the corollary of a genuine faith in God. We do not know with absolute certainty, nor can we readily imagine, how this is to be accomplished. My own suggestion has been that it is through the unfailing reality of what, following Old Testament usage and assisted by Whiteheadian (and Hartshorneian) thought, I have styled 'the divine memory'. To talk in that fashion is not to speak of a kind of meaningless re-enactment of what went on in the creation; it is to speak of a vital, living, and ongoing movement, where God knows and experiences (if that word is, as I believe, appropriate to the divine life) that which has taken place, but knows it and experiences it with a continuing freshness and delight – and, if what has taken place has been evil, with a continuing tinge of sadness and regret – such as must be proper to the chief creative and chief receptive agency who is worshipped and served by God's human children.

Furthermore, just as the concept of purgatory has its value in such a new context, so also does the common Catholic Christian practice of prayers for the departed, as well as the recognition that the great saints are still 'alive in God', in the only way that anybody *can* be thus alive: as an undying reality in the divine memory of the world and of every occasion within that world. Obviously my prayers for the departed will not be effectual in *persuading* God to do what already God must be doing – remembering them once they have been received into the divine life and employing their human accomplishments for the furthering of the divine purpose. But it most certainly will link me with that memory of them, thus establishing a genuine 'communion of saints' in which in the here-and-now we too may share. The recognition that the great saints, above all the Blessed Mother of our Lord, are also still present in God's vital memory, is our way of understanding that God can and still does 'use' them to enrich God's own joy and to further the grand design of God's love. This recognition helps *us*, here in our mortal existence, for it sees that the holy ones are not lost forever but rather, having made their contribution to God, are still through that contribution given the one reward that they hoped for – and the reward that we too may hope for.

What is that reward? It is not 'pie in the sky'; it is life in and with God. St Ignatius Loyola saw this clearly enough when he prayed that he, and all of us, might learn to 'labour and not to ask for any reward, but that of knowing that we do [God's] will'. Thus we return to our main point: God and life with God is the one thing that has supreme importance.

Christian faith – as I have insisted again and again – is God-centred – despite our inveterate (and sinful) human attempts to make God adjectival to our own subjective immortality after death. In the famous Jesuit phrase, all is *ad maiorem gloriam Dei*: 'all is towards the greater glory of God'. If by God's 'glory' we understand a majestic court scene in which God is seated upon a great throne, lording it over the creation and gloating in his divine magnificence, then the phrase suggests ideas that are the exact opposite of the 'Galilean vision' of the Love which is self-giving, gladly receptive, utterly ungrudging in generous openness to all that occurs in the created order. But if we understand God's 'glory' as precisely the divine Love-in-act, with its rejoicing in the joys and its sorrowing with the sadness of God's human children – indeed the glory which is nothing other than the divine generosity, gracious welcome, and unfailing faithfulness in mercy and forgiveness, then the phrase is rich in meaning.

Our value or importance is in relationship to just *that* God. Upon that God's love we can always count. God's receptivity can never be exhausted: God's responsiveness to his children, in any and every circumstance, is our supreme 'dependability'; and God's capacity to use, for further enrichment, any and all that is offered assures us of the worth to be found in whatever is good, true, honourable, lovely, or courageous in our human existence.

The Dean of Chapel in my college in Cambridge often uses this prayer at services when remembrance is made of those who have departed this life: 'Lord, in thy mercy, gather into thy purposes the lives of those we remember before thee, that they may not be lost.' Those words, to my mind, say all that we can need or want. God *always* does that which is for the best; and surely for us men and women that best is for us to be received into God's life and thus to be enabled to make our own limited, finite, doubtless defective, contribution to God's abiding intention for the creation.

An Additional Note:
Addressed to Those Who Mourn

It may be that some readers of this book will feel that its conclusions give what they might think to be small comfort for those who have been bereaved of someone they love and who mourn deeply over their loss. I can understand this feeling on the part of people who have been brought up to accept the conventional notion that heaven will be a place of meeting with those who have died and who wish to have assurance that continuing conscious personal existence after death is guaranteed to us humans. Indeed I myself was brought up with these beliefs; and the adjustment to what I consider to be both a more profoundly Christian and a more rational view was by no means easy. But I came to see that what was important was neither what I had been taught as a child when my brother and sister died at a very early age nor what would provide some immediate comfort to me when (as was bound to happen and of course did happen some years later) my parents also died, leaving me with no close living relations. What *was* important was a conviction that was deeply in accordance with the God-centredness of Christian faith and that could be maintained without special pleading or the use of highly suspect argument. And in this book I have tried to give a clear statement of just that conviction.

None the less, it would be mistaken to think that there is no genuine comfort, no real consolation, in the view presented in these pages. First of all, however, we ought to see that for anyone who understands the order of priorities in Christian faith, the words of St Francis de Sales must be taken very seriously: 'We are to seek the God of consolations rather than the consolations of God.' By this he meant that for a great many people the whole function of their faith is to provide them either with a keen awareness of what God does for them and in them or with a way of escape from the real facts of life. But if God *is* – that is, if the cosmic Love is inescapably *there* and not simply a speculation or wish on the part of us men and women – and if God is also the divine, worshipful, and unsurpassable One who is concerned with and acts for his world in all its richness and variety, then surely the significant thing for us is to focus our attention upon that One. It is not to 'use' God as a way for us to receive creaturely satisfaction of any sort – although of course there is a sense in which we can indeed be satisfied only when we are in conscious relationship with God. We need to have our priorities right, as I have said.

What is more, for any Christian, and indeed for any theist, whatever hope we may have must be *in God*. Unfortunately not a few people take this to be a way of saying that God is the guarantee that what *we* hope for, or think *we* want, will be granted. But to think in this fashion is not to hope in God at all; it is to hope for what we want and then to assume that God is, so to say, the reliable agent who will get it for us or give it to us. The whole point of our discussion in these pages has been to urge that we do indeed put our hope *in God*; it is *God* and God alone, who is our hope, not that which we expect to receive or to have been guaranteed.

In itself that ought to provide great comfort or consolation for those who mourn. The comfort or consolation is not in what may (or may not) happen to us and to those whom we love, once this mortal life is ended. Rather, it is in the sure affirmation of faith that with God and in God, everything is for ever *safe* – and safe in the one way in which it can be enduringly secure, namely in God's valuing and receiving it into the divine life, to be treasured there for ever. The comfort and consolation are given us in the sure conviction that God is always doing 'more than we can ask or think', as the old prayer phrases it; God will do everything possible for us human children, come what may.

At many funerals a phrase is used about our 'committing' to God those whom we have lost. Do we take this phrase as seriously as we should? If we do, we mean that we are then 'giving back' to God the life that has come from God in the first place, in the 'sure and certain hope', as the funeral services also often say, that God cares for the departed one as much as, in fact much more than, we have done and furthermore that God is trustworthy enough to accept and value what has thus been 'committed'.

If our human existence is not that of some supposedly substantial and indestructible soul to whom experiences happen, but is rather those experiences themselves held together in unity and given identity by the awareness and self-awareness which makes it possible for us to say 'I' and 'you', then the enduring reality, which God accepts and values, is precisely that series of events or occasions which go to make us what we are. Are those of such a quality that they can indeed be valued by God, given significance in God's own life, and employed for the furthering of the divine purpose of bringing greater love into existence in more places, in more ways, and at more times? This is the crucial question; it is the question which makes us understand that our day-to-day human life must be lived responsibly and seriously, with due regard for the consequences of our decisions and for what happens as a result of them.

So it is that in my own experiences, I have come to learn that the important thing about those whom I have loved is found in what they have contributed to the ongoing creative advance of God's love in the world. And I can have no doubt, if I earnestly believe that God is unfailing Love, that God too values just those contributions and makes them part of his own unending life. The exact details, *how* this may be done, are veiled from us; the reality itself is given with our faith in God as cosmic Lover.

Some years ago, a memorial service was held for a man whom I had known and loved for a very long time. He was Daniel Day Williams, a gentle and brave man, a great scholar but an even greater person. Those who knew him felt his loss with a terrible poignancy, not least because it came so unexpectedly and without much prior warning. At that service, one of us – not myself but another who had known him well – made some remarks, requested by those who arranged the memorial. In the course of these remarks, this was said: 'Those of us who shared our friend's deep faith in God as Love can have a confidence that nothing that he did, or said, or wrote, or thought can ever be lost. For we believe that God values and treasures and will keep for ever all those acts and words and books and thoughts, keep them for ever in his own everlasting life. So it is that we dare to say that the goodness, the courage, the integrity, the concern, and the love which were our friend – that all these are now, and to all eternity will be, safe in the God whom he and we know to be sheer Love. In that certainty, we can and we do commit our friend to God, in joyful confidence and with the assurance of faith.'

I do not know what the reader may feel; but I can say that for me this was enough, more than enough, to provide comfort and consolation. For our hope is *in God*, the all-merciful and all-loving One, whose care for us who are God's human children is greater than we can grasp or think.

In St Augustine's *Confessions* there is a beautiful passage in which the great African theologian speaks about the death of his beloved friend Alypius. He says that when his friend died, it seemed that half of himself died too, since that friend was so much part of him and had been so much united with him in life. It was as if Augustine had lost part of himself when his friend died. But he goes on to say that he came to see that in truth he had not lost his friend at all, despite the latter's death. For, he writes, 'We can never lose those whom we have loved if we have loved them in God, since we have in fact loved them in the God whom we can never lose.' To love another *in God* is to 'have' that other despite the 'changes and chances of this mortal life', because *in God* that one is loved, known, and kept in all his immediacy; and this means that it is in God, and in God alone, that any genuine hope must be placed. He who is sheer Love, the unsurpassable Love that is divine and everlasting, is our unfailing strength and our ground for confidence, now and always, *in saecula saeculorum*. To him alone we can, and we must, give all praise, honour, thanksgiving, and adoration. Christian faith is utterly theocentric; it is centred in God himself, in God as he discloses himself in the focal event from which that faith takes its origin – Jesus Christ, Man of Nazareth and Lord raised from the dead and abiding for ever in 'the bosom of the Father .